# Article 6

# The Right to Life, Survival and Development

A Commentary on the United Nations Convention
on the Rights of the Child

*Editors*

André Alen, Johan Vande Lanotte, Eugeen Verhellen,
Fiona Ang, Eva Berghmans and Mieke Verheyde

# Article 6

# The Right to Life, Survival and Development

*By*

Manfred Nowak

UN Special Rapporteur on Torture
Director of the Ludwig Boltzmann Institute of Human Rights
at Vienna University

MARTINUS NIJHOFF PUBLISHERS
LEIDEN • BOSTON
2005

This book is printed on acid-free paper.

A Cataloging-in-Publication record for this book is available from the Library of Congress.

Cite as: M. Nowak, "Article 6. The Right to Life, Survival and Development", in: A. Alen, J. Vande Lanotte, E. Verhellen, F. Ang, E. Berghmans and M. Verheyde (Eds.) *A Commentary on the United Nations Convention on the Rights of the Child* (Martinus Nijhoff Publishers, Leiden, 2005).

ISSN 1574-8626
ISBN 90-04-14559-1

# CONTENTS

# LIST OF ABBREVIATIONS

| | |
|---|---|
| ACHPR | African Charter on Human and Peoples' Rights 1981 |
| ACHR | American Convention on Human Rights 1969 |
| ARI | Acute Respiratory Infections |
| Art. | Article |
| CCPR | International Covenant on Civil and Political Rights 1966 |
| CEDAW | Convention on the Elimination of All Forms of Discrimination against Women 1979 |
| CESCR | International Covenant on Economic, Social and Cultural Rights 1966 |
| CRC | Convention on the Rights of the Child 1989 |
| ECHR | European Convention on Human Rights 1950 |
| FGM | Female Genital Mutilation |
| GenC | General Comment |
| ILO | International Labour Organization |
| OP | Optional Protocol |
| ORT | Oral Rehydration Therapy |
| Res. | Resolution |
| SG | Secretary-General |
| UDHR | Universal Declaration of Human Rights 1948 |
| UNICEF | United Nations Children's Fund |
| WHO | World Health Organization |

# AUTHOR BIOGRAPHY

*Manfred Nowak* has been Director of the Ludwig Boltzmann Institute of Human Rights (BIM) at Vienna University since its foundation in 1992. Austrian by nationality, he studied law at the University of Vienna and at Columbia University New York. His professional background includes his functions as Director of the Netherlands Institute of Human Rights (SIM) at the University of Utrecht (1987–1989), as head of the legal department of the Austrian Academy of Public Administration in Vienna (1989–2002), as Olof Palme Professor of Human Rights at the Raoul Wallenberg Institute of Human Rights and Humanitarian Law at the University of Lund (2002–2003) and as Visiting Professor at the European Inter-University Centre for Human Rights and Democratisation (EIUC) in Venice (2004), where he wrote the present article. He also serves or has served as member of the Austrian delegation to the UN Commission on Human Rights (1986–1993), expert member of the UN Working Group on Enforced or Involuntary Disappearances (1993–2001), UN expert on missing persons in the former Yugoslavia (1994–1997), UN expert on legal aspects of enforced disappearances (since 2001), UN Special Rapporteur on Torture (since December 2004), judge at the Human Rights Chamber for Bosnia and Herzegovina in Sarajevo (1996–2003), adviser to the UN High Commissioner for Human Rights on poverty reduction (since 2001), chair of a preventive visiting commission to places of police detention under the authority of the Austrian Minister for Internal Affairs (since 2000), member of the International Commission of Jurists (since 1995) and chairperson of the European Master's Degree in Human Rights and Democratisation (EMA) in Venice (since 2000). He was awarded the UNESCO Prize for the Teaching of Human Rights in 1994 and is author of many books and articles in the field of constitutional law and human rights, including most recently the *Introduction to the International Human Rights Regime* (Leiden/ Boston, Martinus Nijhoff Publishers, 2003), and the *UN Covenant on Civil and Political Rights—CCPR Commentary*, 2nd edition (Kehl/Strasbourg/Arlington, Engel Publishers, 2005).

# TEXT OF ARTICLE 6

ARTICLE 6

1. *States Parties recognize that every child has the inherent right to life.*
2. *States Parties shall ensure to the maximum extent possible the survival and development of the child.*

ARTICLE 6

1. *Les Etats parties reconnaissent que tout enfant a un droit inhérent à la vie.*
2. *Les Etats parties assurent dans toute la mesure possible la survie et le développement de l'enfant.*

CHAPTER ONE

INTRODUCTION*

1. The right to life, survival and development of the child is the most fundamental of all human rights of the child and has been designated by the Committee on the Rights of the Child as one of the four general principles of the Convention on the Rights of the Child (CRC). Without the respect and adequate protection and fulfilment of the right to life, all other rights of the Convention become meaningless.

2. According to the Report of the United Nations Children's Fund (UNICEF) on 'The State of the World's Children 2003', more than *one third of the total world population* (2,16 out of 6,22 billion) are *children, i.e.* persons under the age of 18 years, and roughly 10 per cent of all human beings (613 million) are children under the age of 5 years.[1] More than one third of all the children in the world live in only two countries (India: 402 million, and China: 376 million), whereas less than 10 per cent of all children (190 million) live in industrialized countries, 74 million of which in the United States. Other countries with more than 50 million children include Indonesia (78), Pakistan (69), Bangladesh (63), Nigeria (60) and Brazil (59).

3. The most important indicator for the life, survival, development and well-being of children is the *child (under-5) mortality rate, i.e.* the probability of dying between birth and exactly five years of age expressed per 1,000 live births. In 2001, the under 5 mortality ranking of 193 States revealed enormous differences between rich and poor countries, as the following examples show: Sweden (3), industrialized countries (7), developing countries (89), least developed countries (157), Sub-Saharan Africa (173), Sierra Leone (316). In other words, whereas certain deaths of children are unavoidable, the great majority of child deaths and suffering are the result of preventable causes, above all poverty, armed conflicts, preventable diseases, malnutrition, lack of access to clean water, poor hygienic conditions and

---

* December 2004, with the exception of the references to *USSC Roper v Simmons* under No. 28.

[1] For these and the following figures see UNICEF, The State of the World's Children 2003 (New York, UNICEF, 2002), pp. 83–103. The data refer to the year 2001.

insufficient health and education services. These *causes for the death of more than 10 million children per year are human-made*, and in a world composed of sovereign States, *Governments* bear the *main responsibility* for these deaths. If they do not take sufficient action to protect children against preventable causes of death, they violate the most important of all human rights, the right of children to *life and survival*.

4. The right to life in Article 6 of the CRC goes, however, far beyond the protection of the mere survival of the child. The obligation of States Parties to ensure the development of the child in addition to his or her life and survival illustrates that the right to life has to be interpreted in a comprehensive manner. The *UN Committee on the Rights of the Child* (hereinafter referred to as the CRC Committee or just as the Committee) perceives the *development of the child* as a *holistic concept* similar to the concept of "human development", as defined in Article 1 of the UN Declaration on the Right to Development of 1986. Development is defined therein as a comprehensive process aimed at the full realization of all civil, political, economic, social and cultural rights of the human being. The obligation of States Parties to the CRC to ensure "to the maximum extent possible" the survival and development of the child, therefore, means that States shall create an environment which enables all children under their respective jurisdiction to grow up in a healthy and protected manner, free from fear and want, and to develop their personality, talents and mental and physical abilities to their fullest potential consistent with their evolving capacities. In addition, States also have an obligation in a rapidly globalizing society to provide international co-operation and assistance for the healthy development of children in other countries and regions of our common world, above all, in poor and developing countries.

5. The understanding of the right to life as both a human right of the child and a general principle of the CRC requires an *interpretation of Article 6 which takes into account all the other human rights enshrined in the Convention*. Of particular relevance for the development of the child are the rights to health (Article 24), education (Articles 28 and 29), an adequate standard of living, including nutrition, water, clothing and housing (Article 27), social security (Article 26) and rest, leisure and play (Article 31). The right to life further includes the prohibition of the death penalty (Article 37(a)), the protection of children in armed conflicts (Article 38) and their non-recruitment into the armed forces (2nd OP to the CRC). In addition, the right to life, survival and development of the child entails far-reaching obligations of States to protect children against homicide, infanticide, suicide, pre-

ventable child and infant mortality, harmful traditional practices, such as honour killings and female genital mutilation, violence, exploitation, child labour, trafficking, child prostitution and child pornography, as laid down in various provisions of the CRC, such as Articles 19, 32, 33, 34, 35, 36 as well as the 1st OP to the CRC and ILO Convention No. 182 on Worst Forms of Child Labour.

6. After a detailed comparison with related human rights provisions in the CRC and in other international and regional human rights treaties, the present commentary will discuss the scope of Article 6 in light of the *obligations of States Parties to respect, protect and fulfil* the right to life, survival and development of the child. The interpretation of Article 6 is based on the general rules of interpretation laid down in the Vienna Convention on the Law of Treaties and puts particular emphasis on the *travaux préparatoires*, the practice of the CRC Committee in the State reporting procedure pursuant to Article 44 of the CRC, respective jurisprudence of other human rights monitoring bodies, such as the European Court of Human Rights and the UN Human Rights Committee, and relevant academic literature.

## CHAPTER TWO

## COMPARISON WITH RELATED INTERNATIONAL
## HUMAN RIGHTS PROVISIONS

7. As one of the four general principles of the Convention identified by the Committee, the right to life, development and survival serves as a kind of umbrella clause, which is further defined and elaborated upon in many other provisions of the Convention. While the right to survival has no explicit counterparts in other human rights treaties,[2] the right to life as one of the fundamental human rights of the so-called "first generation" can be found in all general, universal as well as regional, instruments on civil and political rights. Similarly, the right to development as a typical example of the so-called "third generation" figures prominently in modern human rights instruments dealing with so-called solidarity rights. The relationship between the general right to development and the more specific right of the child to a healthy development will be further explained below.

8. The most important provisions that guarantee the *right to life* are Articles 3 of the UDHR, 6 of the CCPR, 2 of the ECHR, 4 of the ACHR and 4 of the ACHPR. While the Universal Declaration links the right to life to the right to personal liberty and security, the African Charter puts it under the umbrella of the inviolability of human beings and connects it to the right to personal integrity. The Covenant as well as the European and American Convention, on the other hand, treat the right to life as a separate provision at the beginning of the respective catalogues of civil and political rights and contain more or less detailed provisions on the death penalty which have later been supplemented by the 2nd OP to the CCPR, the 6th and 13th AP to the ECHR and a Protocol of 1990 to the ACHR, all aiming at the abolition of capital punishment. The general prohibition to impose the death penalty for crimes committed by children (persons below eighteen years of age, as defined in Article 1 of the CRC) is already contained in Article 6(5) of the CCPR and Article 4(5) of the ACHR and has been reconfirmed in specific

---

[2] Only Article 5(2) of the African Charter on the Rights and Welfare of the Child of 1990, which is modelled on Article 6 of the CRC, contains an obligation of States to ensure the 'survival, protection and development of the child'.

instruments on the rights of the child. Whereas Article 5(3) of the African Charter on the Rights and Welfare of the Child stipulates this prohibition in the context of the right to life, Article 37(a) of the CRC regulates the prohibition of capital punishment in the context of the rights to personal liberty and security.

9. In addition to the obligation of States to *respect* the right to life, Article 6(1) of the CCPR, Article 2(1) of the ECHR and Article 4(1) of the ACHR also contain an explicit provision that the right to life shall be *protected* by law. While the Covenant and the American Convention, apart from detailed limitations in respect of capital punishment, only contain a general prohibition of arbitrary deprivation of life, more detailed examples of a non-arbitrary deprivation can be found in Article 2(2) of the European Convention, *i.e.* when death results from absolutely necessary use of force for certain law enforcement purposes. The right to life is treated as a non-derogable right in Articles 4(2) CCPR, 27(2) ACHR and 15(2) ECHR, but only the latter provision makes an explicit exception in respect of deaths resulting from lawful acts of war. A similar obligation of States to ensure respect for the rules of international humanitarian law applicable in armed conflicts can be found in Article 38 of the CRC, but the prohibition of recruiting children into the armed forces has been limited to children below fifteen years of age. Only States Parties to the 2nd OP on the involvement of children in armed conflict have undertaken obligations not to compulsorily recruit children between 15 and 18 years of age into their armed forces and to raise the minimum age for the voluntary recruitment of children.

10. The most prominent provisions on the *right to development* are Article 22 of the ACHPR and the United Nations Declaration on the Right to Development. While the African Charter guarantees the right to development and other solidarity rights, such as the "right to a general satisfactory environment favourable to their development" in Article 24 as a purely collective right of peoples, Article 1 of the 1986 UN Declaration defines the right to development as an "inalienable human right by virtue of which every human being and all peoples are entitled to participate in, contribute to, and enjoy economic, social, cultural and political development, in which all human rights and fundamental freedoms can be fully realized". Although Article 6 of the CRC does not speak of a general right of the child to development, but instead of the obligation of States to ensure the *development of the child*, there can be no doubt that the right to survival and development of the child was drafted with the aim of establishing a link between the rights of children, in particular the right to life and survival, and the devel-

opment discourse of that time.[3] The right to development, as defined in the 1986 UN Declaration, is the most important legal expression of the link between the human rights and the development discourses. In other words, the various provisions of the CRC which refer to the development of the child shall also be interpreted in the spirit of the overall concept of human development, as it emerged during the late 1980s, and the concept of the development of the child, as defined in the CRC, might be used for better understanding the notion and aims of human development, as expressed in the inalienable human right to development.

11. The contents of the development of the child in Article 6 of the CRC are further defined, *e.g.*, in Articles 5, 18, 20, 23(3), 24, 27, 28, 29, 31 and 39 of the CRC. According to Article 18, both parents have common responsibilities for the upbringing and development of the child, and States shall render appropriate assistance to parents in this respect and, pursuant to Article 5, shall respect the rights and responsibilities of parents to provide, in a manner consistent with the *evolving capacities of the child*, appropriate direction and guidance. All provisions aimed at family reunification and preventing separation of children from their parents, such as Articles 9 to 11, underline this basic concept that the parents have the primary responsibility for the development of the child in conformity with the evolving capacities of the child. Should a child, temporarily or permanently, be deprived of his or her family environment, States Parties are obliged under Article 20 to provide special protection and assistance, such as foster placement. Article 23 contains specific State obligations in relation to mentally or physically disabled children which shed further light on the minimum conditions and aims of the child's development. According to Article 23(3), State assistance shall be 'designed to ensure that the disabled child has effective access to and receives education, training, health care services, rehabilitation services, preparation for employment and recreation opportunities in a manner conducive to the child's achieving the fullest possible social integration and individual development, including his or her cultural and spiritual development'. This list of selected rights conducive to the child's development is in fact relevant for all children. First of all, the right of the child to the enjoyment of the highest attainable standard of *health* (Articles 24 and 25), which contains an explicit obligation of States to diminish infant and child mortality, constitutes the most important precondition

---

[3] On the *travaux préparatoires* of Article 6 see *infra*, III.1.

for the right to life, survival and development of the child and is, therefore, most directly linked to Article 6. Secondly, the right of every child to a '*standard of living* adequate for the child's physical, mental, spiritual, moral and social development' (Article 27), which contains specific rights to nutrition (food), clothing and housing, is equally important for the protection of the right to life, survival and development of the child, and Article 27(2) reaffirms the primary responsibility of the parents to secure the 'conditions of living necessary for the child's development'. Thirdly, the right to *education* (Articles 28 and 29), which shall be directed to the 'development of the child's personality, talents and mental and physical abilities to their fullest potential' as well as to the 'development of respect for human rights and fundamental freedoms', is the most important tool for facilitating the child's development in accordance with its 'evolving capacities'. Closely related to the right to education is the explicit right of the child to *rest and leisure*, to engage in play and recreational activities appropriate to the age of the child and to participate freely in cultural life and the arts (Article 31). Finally, States shall take all appropriate measures to promote physical and psychological *recovery and social reintegration* of a child victim of any form of neglect, exploitation, abuse, torture or armed conflicts (Article 39). Such recovery and reintegration shall take place in an environment which fosters the health, self-respect and dignity of the child.

12. The above mentioned *economic, social and cultural rights* most directly linked to the survival and development of the child are, of course, also contained in general instruments on this so-called 'second generation' of human rights, such as Articles 11 to 13 CESCR. In addition, Article 10 of the Covenant recognizes the widest possible protection to the family, which is the 'natural and fundamental group unit of society, particularly for its establishment and while it is responsible for the care and education of dependent children'. Special protection should be accorded to mothers during a reasonable period before and after childbirth, and children should be protected from economic and social exploitation. 'Their employment in work harmful to their morals or health or dangerous to life or likely to hamper their normal development should be punishable by law'. Similar provisions for the protection of the family and children can also be found in Articles 23 and 24 CCPR.

13. In addition to the prohibition of torture, capital punishment and life imprisonment in Article 37(a), the CRC contains a number of specific State obligations to protect children against various forms of *violence and exploitation* which endanger the survival and healthy development of the child.

Most importantly, reference shall be made to the protection of children from all forms of violence, abuse, neglect, maltreatment or exploitation, including sexual abuse (Article 19), from economic exploitation and work that is likely to be hazardous or to 'interfere with the child's education, or to be harmful to the child's health or physical, mental, spiritual, moral or social development' (Article 32), from the illicit use of narcotic drugs (Article 33), from all forms of sexual exploitation and abuse, including child prostitution and pornography (Article 34), from abduction, sale and trafficking (Article 35), and from other forms of exploitation (Article 36). These important provisions have been supplemented and further developed by the adoption of the 1st OP on the sale of children, child prostitution and child pornography. In addition, the Minimum Age Convention, the Worst Forms of Child Labour Convention and other ILO conventions protect children from economic exploitation.

CHAPTER THREE

SCOPE OF ARTICLE 6

1. *Travaux Préparatoires*

14. Neither the earlier Declarations of the Right of the Child nor the original draft Convention submitted by Poland in 1978 contained a right of the child to life. But Article I of the League of Nations Declaration of the Rights of the Child 1924 provided that the child must be given the means requisite for its normal *development*, both materially and spiritually.[4] This provision was further elaborated in Principle 2 of the UN Declaration of the Rights of the Child 1959, which reads as follows:[5]

> 'The child shall enjoy special protection, and shall be given opportunities and facilities, by law and by other means, to enable him to develop physically, mentally, morally, spiritually and socially in a healthy and normal manner and in conditions of freedom and dignity. In the enactment of laws for this purpose, the best interests of the child shall be the paramount consideration.'

15. The entire text of Principle 2 of the 1959 Declaration was literally repeated in Article II of the draft Convention on the Rights of the Child, submitted by *Poland* to the UN Commission on Human Rights on 7 February 1978.[6] In Res. 20 (XXXIV) of 8 March 1978, the Commission requested the Secretary-General to invite Member States, specialized agencies, inter-governmental and non-governmental organizations to communicate their views, observations and suggestions on the draft Convention. Many Governments and organizations observed in their replies that the wording of a binding Convention should be much more concrete and specific than that of the Declaration, which had been formulated twenty years earlier.[7] In addition,

---

[4] For the text, see G. Van Bueren (ed.), *International Documents on Children*, 2nd ed. (The Hague/Boston/London, Martinus Nijhoff Publishers, 1998), p. 3.

[5] *Ibid.*, p. 5.

[6] For the text, see the Annex to Commission Res. 20 (XXXIV) of 8 March 1978 (UN Doc. E/1978/34), chap. XXVI, sect. A. The text of the draft Convention and other relevant documents on the drafting of the CRC are reproduced in S. Detrick (ed.), *The United Nations Convention on the Rights of the Child, A Guide to the 'Travaux Préparatoires'* (Dordrecht/Boston/London, Martinus Nijhoff Publishers, 1992).

[7] For a summary of these replies see the report of the SG in UN Doc. E/CN.4/1324, reproduced in Detrick, *supra* note 6, p. 36 *et seq.*

the Convention should be elaborated with due regard for the current problems confronting children.[8] On 5 October 1979, Poland submitted a revised draft Convention which, however, no longer contained an explicit provision on the development of the child. The principle of the 'best interests of the child' can be found in Article 3(1) of the revised draft Convention. In addition, Article 3(2) established the obligation of States, similar to those in Article 24(1) of the CCPR, 'to ensure the child such protection and care as his status requires, taking due account of the various stages of his development in family environment and in social relations'.[9] The physical, mental and moral development of the child is, however stressed in Articles 13 and 15, *i.e.* in the context of the right to health care and the right to a standard of living 'adequate for his healthy and normal physical, mental and moral development in every phase of the child's development'.[10] This revised draft formed the basis for the further work in the inter-sessional Working Group during the following decade.

16. It was only in 1988 that *India* submitted a proposal for the insertion of a new Article 1 *bis*:[11]

'The States Parties to the present Convention undertake to create an environment, within their capacities and constitutional processes, which ensures, to the maximum extent possible, the survival and healthy development of the child.'

In the ensuing discussions, the representative of India stressed the need for a separate *right of children to survival*, bearing in mind that many children died from preventable causes. This right should be supplemented by the notion of healthy development as many children only survived in very poor conditions. Other delegations criticized, however, that the concept of survival was not defined in international law. Since life and survival seemed to be complementary and not mutually exclusive, the representative of *Italy* proposed to insert a specific provision on the *right to life*, similar to Article 3 of the UDHR and Article 6 of the CCPR. Others observed, however, that the Working Group had agreed not to reopen the discussion concerning the moment at which life begins. It was also stated that the right to survival

---

[8] See also the first report of the inter-sessional open-ended Working Group on the Convention on the Rights of the Child submitted to the Commission in 1979 (UN Doc. E/1979/36), chap. IX, reproduced in S. Detrick, *o.c.* (note 6), p. 89.

[9] UN Doc. E/CN.4/1349: see S. Detrick, *o.c.* (note 6), p. 96.

[10] *Ibid.*, p. 98.

[11] UN Doc. E/CN.4/WG.1/WP.13. For this and the following, see the report of the Working Group (UN Doc. E/CN.4/1988/28), reproduced in S. Detrick, *o.c.* (note 6), p. 120.

carried with it a more positive connotation than the right to life, meaning the right to have positive steps taken to prolong the life of the child. In summing up the debate, the Chairman-Rapporteur stated that the right to life should be included as a priority before other rights of the child. The approach to the right to life in the Covenants was rather negative, while that of the draft Convention should be positive and should take into account economic, social and cultural conditions.

17. On the proposal of the Chair, a small *drafting group*, consisting of Argentina, Bulgaria, India, Italy, Norway, UNICEF and the United Kingdom, submitted the following compromise text:

> '1. The States Parties to the present Convention recognize that every child has the inherent right to life.
> 2. States Parties shall ensure, to the maximum extent possible, the survival and development of the child.'

This compromise formulation was adopted by the Working Group in 1988.[12] One year later the representative of *Venezuela*, who had already earlier expressed objections to the concept of survival as, in her view, it would diminish the concept of the right to life conferred on all human beings in existing international instruments, proposed to replace the word 'survival' by 'healthy growth'.[13] The representative of the World Health Organization (WHO) maintained, however, that the term 'survival' had a special meaning within the United Nations context, especially for his organization and UNICEF. 'Survival' included growth monitoring, oral rehydration and disease control, breastfeeding, immunization, child spacing, food and female literacy; the term 'growth' represented only a part of the concept of 'survival' and the change would be a step backwards from standards already accepted. Delegates from Australia, Norway, Italy, Sweden and India also stated their preference for the retention of the word 'survival', and the representative of Italy indicated that in the language of international organizations the two words 'survival' and 'development' had come to acquire the special meaning of ensuring the child's survival in order to realize the full development of his or her personality, both from the material and spiritual points of view. After the representative of Venezuela withdrew her amendment, the Working Group at second reading confirmed the text of

[12] UN Doc. E/CN.4/1988/WG.1/WP.1/Rev.2, p. 6; see S. Detrick, *o.c.* (note 6), p. 122.
[13] UN Doc. E/CN.4/1989/WG.1/WP.10; see S. Detrick, *o.c.* (note 6), p. 122.

Article 6 as adopted already in 1988.[14] This formulation remained unchanged in the Commission and General Assembly.

18. One can conclude from the *travaux préparatoires* that *paras. 1 and 2 of Article 6 are interrelated* and interdependent. At the beginning, special measures of protection to ensure the *healthy development* of the child were in the foreground. On the initiative of India, the right of children to a healthy development was supplemented by a right to *survival*. Both concepts were interpreted in the sense which international organizations, such as UNICEF and the WHO, had accorded to it in the context of the human development discourse of the late 1980s. As the CRC is a human rights instrument, Italy insisted that these terms should be combined with the traditional language of human rights, above all the right to *life*. But it was made clear that the right to life had to be interpreted in a comprehensive manner. In particular, the approach to the right to life should be positive in the sense of State obligations to ensure the survival and development of the child by the adoption of *positive measures*. The *travaux préparatoires* also clearly show that the right to life and development is closely connected to and further defined by other rights and principles of the Convention, such as the principle of the 'best interests of the child' in Article 3 as well as the rights to health, an adequate standard of living and education in Articles 24, 27, 28 and 29 of the CRC.

### 2. Article 6 as one of the General Principles of the CRC

19. The right to life has properly been characterized by the Human Rights Committee as the supreme human right, since without effective guarantee of this right, all other rights of the human being would be devoid of meaning.[15] The CRC Committee went one step further in according specific significance to the right to life in the CRC. Already during its first session in October 1991, in adopting *General Guidelines regarding the form and content of initial reports* to be submitted by States Parties, it identified *four general prin-*

---

[14] UN Doc. E/CN.4/1989/29/Rev.1, p. 5; see S. Detrick, *o.c.* (note 6), p. 123.
[15] See *e.g.* Human Rights Committee, *General Comment No. 6: the Right to Life* (UN Doc. HRI/GEN/1/Rev.7, 1982), para. 1 and *General Comment No. 14: Nuclear Weapons and the Right to Life* (UN Doc. HRI/GEN/1/Rev.7, 1984), para. 1 in relation to Article 6 of the CCPR. On the significance and interpretation of this provision see M. Nowak, *UN Covenant on Civil and Political Rights—CCPR Commentary*, 2nd ed. (Kehl/Strasbourg/ Arlington, N.P. Engel Publishers, 2004), pp. 121–122.

*ciples* of the Convention: non-discrimination (Article 2), the best interests of the child (Article 3), the right to life, survival and development (Article 6), and respect for the views of the child (Article 12).[16] In addition to providing relevant information on the implementation of these four provisions, States Parties were also encouraged to provide relevant information on the application of these principles in the implementation of articles listed elsewhere in these guidelines.[17] In the *General Guidelines for periodic reports* adopted in 1996, the Committee reaffirmed these four principles and, in respect of Article 6, encouraged States Parties to 'describe specific measures taken to guarantee the child's right to life and to create an environment conducive to ensuring to the maximum extent possible the survival and development of the child, including physical, mental, spiritual, moral, psychological and social development, in a manner compatible with human dignity, and to prepare the child for an individual life in a free society'.[18] This interpretation corresponds to the meaning accorded to this provision by its drafters as can be seen from the *travaux préparatoires*.[19] In the following, the Committee drew the attention of States Parties to a few specific aspects of the right to life:[20]

> 'Information should also be provided on the measures taken to ensure the registration of the deaths of the children, the causes of death and, where appropriate, investigation and reporting on such deaths, as well as on the measures adopted to prevent children's suicide and monitor its incidence and to ensure the survival of children at all ages, including adolescents, and the prevention of risks to which that group may be particularly exposed (for example, sexually transmitted diseases, street violence). Please provide relevant disaggregated data, including on the number of suicides among children.'

20. In the fall session of 2003, the Committee adopted a *General Comment on general measures of implementation of the CRC,* which are intended to promote the full enjoyment of all CRC rights by all children, through legislation, the establishment of coordinating and monitoring bodies—governmental and independent—comprehensive data collection, awareness-raising and training and the development and implementation of appropriate policies, services and programmes.[21] In this context, the Committee stressed that the

---

[16]  See UN Doc. CRC/C/5, para. 13.
[17]  *Ibid.*, para. 14.
[18]  UN Doc. CRC/C/58, para. 40.
[19]  See *supra*, III.1.
[20]  UN Doc. CRC/C/58, para. 41.
[21]  CRC Committee, *General Comment No. 5: General Measures of Implementation of the Convention on the Rights of the Child.* (UN Doc. CRC/GC/2003/5, 2003), para. 9.

development of *a children's rights perspective* through Government, parliament and the judiciary is required for effective implementation of the whole Convention and, 'in particular, in the light of the following articles of the Convention identified by the Committee as general principles:

> 'Article 6: the child's inherent right to life and States parties' obligation to ensure to the maximum extent possible the survival and development of the child. The Committee expects States to interpret 'development' in its broadest sense as a holistic concept, embracing the child's physical, mental, spiritual, moral, psychological and social development. Implementation measures should be aimed at achieving the optimal development for all children.'[22]

21. In fairly critical comments on the draft General Comment on general measures, the well-known children's rights expert *Bruce Abramson* observed that the concept of 'general principles' has turned out to be a stumbling block in the reporting procedure as it has led to disorganization, misunderstandings of CRC rights and to the problem of *'front-loading', i.e.* the habit of using this cluster 'to ask questions that really should be asked in the clusters that pertain to the various substantive rights'.[23] He identifies the root of the front-loading problem in the reporting guidelines. The State frontloads its report in response to the guidelines, and then the Committee's dialogue follows the established pattern. Even more seriously, speaking in terms of 'general principles' is, according to *Abramson*, an 'extremely weak way to talk about the legal obligations of States under the CRC: it undermines the concept of rights, and it misrepresents the state's legal obligations'.[24] More specifically, calling Article 6 a 'general principle' would undermine it as a right and would lead to superficiality. 'In reading the state reports, for example, one does not see article 6 playing any significant role in the substantive rights clusters. Calling it a general principle turns a human right into a superficial cliché.'[25]

22. There is indeed a certain danger that States report on the right to life only in the context of the chapter on 'general principles' and, thereby, misrepresent its significance as an independent substantive right. Similarly, in its country-specific *Concluding Observations on State reports*, the CRC Committee

---

[22] *Ibid.*, para. 12.
[23] B. Abramson, 'Two stumbling blocks to CRC monitoring: the four "general principles" and "The definition of the child", Annex to Comments on the "General Comment on General Measures (Second Draft)"', 1 September 2003 (conference paper).
[24] *Ibid.*
[25] *Ibid.*

tends to ignore specific problems and difficulties regarding the implementation of the right to life by referring to Article 6 primarily in the context of general remarks on the significance of the four general principles.[26] On the other hand, it seems undisputed that the concept of 'survival and best possible development of the child', which has been linked to the right to life in Article 6, is crucial to the implementation of the whole Convention. Its full significance only becomes clear if one interprets it in close relationship with a considerable number of other CRC rights, above all the rights to health, food and education.[27] The identification of four general principles of the Convention, including the right to life, survival and development of the child, definitely serves the purpose of highlighting to States the fundamental values underlying the Convention, of ensuring a common philosophical approach to the broad spectrum of areas addressed by the Convention, and of defining decisive criteria to assess the progress made in the implementation of a children's rights approach.[28]

### 3. The 'Inherent' Right to Life

23. The right to life is the only right in the CRC described as inherent.[29] This expression has been taken over from Article 6(1) of the CCPR, where it was adopted with the intention to give expression to the natural-law basis of the right to life.[30] The Human Rights Committee concluded from this formulation, *e.g.*, that the right to life must not be interpreted restrictively[31] and that States Parties are under a specific obligation to ensure this right

---

[26] See *e.g.* the collection of these country-specific observations in L. Holmström (ed.), *Concluding Observations of the UN Committee on the Rights of the Child* (The Hague, Martinus Nijhoff Publishers, 2000), pp. 25, 33, 36, 43, 53, 119, 134, 175, 188, 198, 222, 234, 253, 255, 271, 297, 305, 306, 311, 317, 320, 331, 333, 353, 377, 391, 394, 461, 515.

[27] See *supra*, II.

[28] On the purpose and merits of these four general principles see *e.g.*, M. Santos Pais, *A Human Rights Conceptual Framework for UNICEF* (Florence, UNICEF International Child Development Centre, 1999), p. 9; R. Hodgkin, P. Newell, *Implementation Handbook for the Convention on the Rights of the Child*, Rev. ed. (New York, UNICEF, 2002), pp. 95–106; S. Detrick, A Commentary on the United Nations Convention on the Rights of the Child (The Hague/Boston/London, Martinus Nijhoff Publishers, 1999), p. 67 *et seq.*; M. Nowak, *Introduction to the International Human Rights Regime* (Leiden/Boston, Martinus Nijhoff Publishers, 2003), pp. 92–93; H. Sax, 'Artikel 6: Recht auf Leben und bestmögliche Entwicklung', in *UNICEF Praxishandbuch Kinderrechtskonvention* (not yet published).

[29] *Cf.* G. Van Bueren, *The International Law on the Rights of the Child* (Dordrecht/Boston/London, Martinus Nijhoff Publishers, 1998), p. 303.

[30] *Cf.* M. Nowak, *o.c.* (note 15), p. 122.

[31] See Human Rights Committee, *o.c.* (note 15), paras. 1, 5.

with adequate *positive measures*. The drafting history of Article 6 of the CRC and the interrelationship between the right to life and the concept of survival and development of the child reinforces the obligation of States to adopt specific measures to ensure the best possible and healthy development of children living on their territory. For example, a State Party with a high infant mortality rate is under a duty to create and maintain cost-effective health programmes aimed at preventing life-threatening diseases for children.[32] Finally, the inherent character of the right to life can be interpreted as an indicator for the *non-derogable nature* of this right even in times of war and public emergencies threatening the life of the nation,[33] and as an indicator for its recognition as *jus cogens* under international law.[34]

24. In order to clearly distinguish the negative duty of States not to interfere arbitrarily with the right to life from their obligations to take comprehensive legislative, administrative and other positive measures to ensure, to the maximum extent possible, the inherent and indivisible rights to life, survival and optimal development of children, the following survey will be structured according to the generally accepted trias of States' obligations to respect, fulfil and protect these rights.[35]

### 4. *Obligation to Respect the Right to Life*

25. The obligation of States Parties to respect the right to life refers to the traditional *obligation to refrain from State interference*, provided the latter is not admissible under any relevant legal limitation clause. Any unjustified interference amounts to a violation of the right to life. In general human rights treaty law, the right to life, although a non-derogable right, is not considered as an absolute human right. In addition to the death penalty, general human rights treaties also allow for other cases of killing by State security forces, as long as such interference is not 'arbitrary'[36] and does

---

[32] G. Van Bueren, *o.c.* (note 29), p. 303.

[33] Although the CRC does not contain an explicit emergency clause, the non-derogable character of the right to life follows from various provisions in general human rights treaty law (Article 4(2) of the CCPR, Article 15(2) of the ECHR, Article 27(2) of the ACHR).

[34] See *e.g.* Human Rights Committee, *General Comment No. 24: Reservations to the Covenant or Optional Protocols or Declarations under Art. 41 of the Covenant* (UN Doc. HRI/GEN/1/Rev.7, 1994), para. 8.

[35] On the theoretical background of this trias of obligations see *e.g.* M. Nowak, *o.c.* (note 28), pp. 23–30 and pp. 48–53.

[36] Article 6(1) of the CCPR, Article 4(1) of the ACHR. On the concept of arbitrary deprivation of life see M. Nowak, *o.c.* (note 15), pp. 127–133.

result from an 'absolutely necessary use of force' for certain law enforcement purposes.[37] Article 6(1) of the CRC does not contain any similar limitation clause. The question, therefore, arises as to which extent the limitation clauses in general human rights treaties apply to children.

### 4.1. *Death Penalty*

26. Despite a clear trend in international human rights law towards abolition and towards recognizing that capital punishment, as corporal punishment, constitutes cruel, inhuman and degrading punishment prohibited under international law,[38] there still remain a considerable number of retentionist States, including powerful States such as the United States and China, who not only continue to practice capital punishment but who also maintain that this cruel punishment is compatible with human dignity and other minimum standards of international law and civilized behaviour. There is no other issue which would better illustrate the increasing cultural and political gap between the United States and Europe in approaching human rights and justice.

27. One of the compromises in limiting the application of the death penalty, agreed upon by the drafters of Article 6 of the CCPR during the 1950s and 1960s, was the absolute prohibition of capital punishment in juvenile justice laid down in Article 6(5) of the CCPR: 'Sentence of death shall not be imposed for crimes committed by persons below eighteen years of age and shall not be carried out on pregnant women.' This approach of an absolute prohibition was also adopted in Article 4(5) of the ACHR and Article 37(a) of the CRC, which establishes an explicit link between capital punishment, torture and other cruel, inhuman or degrading treatment or punishment:

> 'No child shall be subjected to torture or other cruel, inhuman or degrading treatment or punishment. Neither capital punishment nor life imprisonment without possibility of release shall be imposed for offences committed by persons below eighteen years of age.'[39]

---

[37] Article 2(2) of the ECHR: For the application of Article 2 of the ECHR to children see U. Kilkelly, The Child and the European Convention on Human Rights (Dartmouth, Ashgate Publishing Company, 1999), pp. 140–149.

[38] See *e.g.* the landmark judgment of the South African Constitutional Court of 6 June 1995 in *State v. Makwanyane and Mchunu*, Case No. CCT/3/94. On the trend towards abolition see W.A.H. Schabas, *The Abolition of the Death penalty in International Law*, 3rd ed. (Cambridge, Cambridge University Press, 2002); M. Nowak, *o.c.* (note 15), pp. 133–138 and pp. 168–172.

[39] For the interpretation of this provision see the CRC Commentary contribution on Article 37 by W. Schabas and H. Sax.

28.  In its General Comment on reservations adopted in November 1994, the Human Rights Committee concluded that the prohibition to impose the death penalty on juveniles constitutes *customary international law* and may, therefore, not be subject to any reservations.[40] The fact that Article 37(a) of the CRC has been ratified, without any reservation, by 192 States underlines this conclusion. The *United States*, which is not yet a party to the CRC, when ratifying the CCPR, however, reserved the right 'to impose capital punishment on any person (other than a pregnant woman) duly convicted under existing or future laws permitting the imposition of capital punishment, including such punishment for crimes committed by persons below eighteen years of age'.[41] Since eleven European States Parties to the Covenant objected to this reservation as being incompatible with the object and purpose of the Covenant, since the Human Rights Committee expressed a strong and unanimous opinion that this reservation was invalid, and since the US is one of very few remaining offenders of the prohibition on juvenile executions today,[42] the customary law nature of the prohibition of the death penalty in juvenile justice has not been challenged by this invalid US reservation.

29.  Although the States Parties to the CRC seem today to comply, in principle, with the absolute prohibition on juvenile execution, the CRC Committee has repeatedly emphasized that it is not enough that capital punishment is not applied to children in practice. Its prohibition regarding children must be confirmed in legislation.[43]

### 4.2. *Armed Conflict*

30.  Armed conflicts, both of an international and non-international character, continue to represent the greatest threat to human life. Since 1990, over 2 million children have been killed and 6 million have been seriously injured in wars.[44] The question, therefore, arises whether all these killings

---

[40]  Human Rights Committee, *o.c.* (note 34), GenC 24/52, para. 8.

[41]  On this issue cf. M. Nowak, *o.c.* (note 15), p. 145 with further references.

[42]  See in this respect W.A.H. Schabas, *o.c.* (note 38), p. 138, who alleges that the US might 'perhaps' even remain as the sole offender. Recent data, compiled by Amnesty International, show that execution of child offenders also takes place in Iran, China, DRC and Pakistan. See <http://www.amnesty.org>. Very recently, the US Supreme Court has declared the death penalty for minor constitutional in *Roper v Simmons* (2005), No. 03.633.

[43]  On the practice of the CRC Committee see R. Hodgkin, P. Newell, *o.c.* (note 28), pp. 99 and 547.

[44]  *Cf.* UNICEF, *o.c.* (note 1), p. 78.

during armed conflicts constitute a violation of the right to life under Article 6 of the CRC. While international humanitarian law distinguishes between combatants and persons taking no active part in the hostilities (civilians, prisoners of war, wounded and sick soldiers and other members of the armed forces who have laid down their arms or who are placed *hors de combat*) by explicitly permitting intentional killing only in relation to combatants, international human rights law, which applies both in times of peace and war, does not make any such distinction. The killing of soldiers, therefore, constitutes a violation of the right to life unless it can be justified by an explicit limitation or derogation clause. The CRC does not contain any derogation clause, and the derogation clauses in Article 4(2) of the CCPR and 27(2) of the ACHR do not allow any derogation from the right to life even in time of public emergency which threatens the life of the nation, such as an armed conflict. On the other hand, Article 15(2) of the ECHR makes an explicit exception to the non-derogability of the right to life 'in respect of deaths resulting from lawful acts of war'. In other words, the killing of combatants in accordance with international humanitarian law must also be interpreted as being in conformity with Article 2 of the ECHR under the condition that the respective State has made a respective derogation in accordance with Article 15 of the ECHR.

31. A similar interpretation should also apply to the term 'arbitrarily' in Articles 6(1) of the CCPR and 4(1) of the ACHR. The intentional killing of soldiers, which does not violate international humanitarian law, as laid down, above all, in the 1949 Geneva Conventions and its 1977 Additional Protocols, shall not be interpreted as an arbitrary deprivation of life and constitutes, therefore, an interference with the right to life that can be justified as non-arbitrary with reference to international humanitarian law.[45] Although the CRC neither contains the word 'arbitrarily' in Article 6 nor an explicit derogation clause in times of war and public emergency, this interpretation shall, in principle, also be applied to Article 6 of the CRC.

32. The decisive question is, therefore, whether the killing of children during armed conflicts can be regarded as 'deaths resulting from lawful acts of war'. Does international humanitarian law allow for the killing of children? Since the exception from the protection of the right to life only applies to combatants, the question in fact boils down to the question whether children can be lawful combatants. International humanitarian law, in principle,

---

[45] *Cf.* in this respect M. Nowak, *o.c.* (note 15), pp. 125–126.

protects only children who have not attained the age of 15 years from recruitment into the armed forces and from participation in hostilities.[46] Attempts of Sweden and other States during the drafting of Article 38 of the CRC aimed at raising the minimum age to 18 years failed because of the opposition of the United States, in particular.[47] Consequently, Article 38(2) of the CRC obliges States only to take all 'feasible measures' to ensure that under 15 year-old children do not take a 'direct' part in hostilities and, therefore, applies a standard which is even lower than that of Article 4(3)(c) of Protocol II to the Geneva Conventions which, for non-international conflicts, provides more categorically that children under the age of 15 'shall neither be recruited in the armed forces or groups nor allowed to take part in hostilities'.[48] When ratifying the CRC, a number of States Parties made declarations which expressed concern that Article 38 did not prohibit the involvement in hostilities and the recruitment into armed forces of all children, *i.e.* persons under the age of 18.[49] Such a provision is, *e.g.*, contained in Article 22(2) of the African Charter on the Rights and Welfare of the Child, which was adopted only one year after the CRC and which reads as follows: 'States Parties to the present Charter shall take all necessary measures to ensure that no child[50] shall take a direct part in hostilities and refrain in particular, from recruiting any child.'

33.   From the beginning, the CRC Committee expressed the opinion that the CRC, taken as a whole, requires protection of all children under 18 from recruitment into the armed forces and from direct or indirect involvement in hostilities.[51] The Committee was also the driving force behind the drafting of an *Optional Protocol to the CRC on the involvement of children in armed conflict*, which was adopted in May 2000 and entered into force in February 2002.[52] Article 1 obliges States Parties to take all feasible measures to ensure that members of their armed forces who have not attained the age of 18 years do not take a direct part in hostilities. Article 2 prohibits the com-

---

[46]   See Article 77(2) of Protocol I and Article 4(3)(c) of Protocol II to the Geneva Conventions of 1949.

[47]   *Cf. e.g.* S. Detrick, *o.c.* (note 6), pp. 502–517; S. Detrick, *o.c.* (note 28), pp. 645–665.

[48]   See also G. Van Bueren, *o.c.* (note 29), pp. 334–336; R. Hodgkin, P. Newell, *o.c.* (note 28), p. 514.

[49]   *Cf.* R. Hodgkin, P. Newell, *o.c.* (note 28), pp. 517–518.

[50]   According to Article 2, a child means every human being below the age of 18 years.

[51]   See R. Hodgkin, P. Newell, *o.c.* (note 28), pp. 517–528.

[52]   GA Res. 54/263 of 25 May 2000, entry into force on 12 February 2002. See also UNICEF/Coalition to Stop the Use of Child Soldiers, Guide to the Optional Protocol on the involvement of children in armed conflict (New York, UNICEF 2003).

pulsory recruitment of children under 18, and Article 3 obliges States to raise in years the minimum age for the voluntary recruitment of children from 15 to 18, bearing in mind that persons under 18 are entitled to special protection.

34. Taking the recent trend in international law against the recruitment and use of child soldiers into account as well as the need to interpret the CRC in a holistic and systematic manner, including the principle of the best interests of the child, it seems difficult to maintain that the intentional killing of child soldiers in combat could be considered as a death 'resulting from lawful acts of war' in the sense of Article 15(2) of the ECHR. The recruitment of child soldiers, their direct or indirect participation in armed conflicts, and at least the intentional killing of child soldiers during combat must, therefore, be considered as an arbitrary deprivation of their right to life in Article 6 of the CCPR and a violation of the right of every child to life, survival and development under Article 6 of the CRC.

35. It is also interesting to note in this context that the Human Rights Committee already in 1982 derived from Article 6 of the CCPR the 'supreme duty' on States to prevent war, genocide and other acts of mass violence causing arbitrary loss of life.[53] Two years later, the Committee designated the designing, testing, manufacturing, possession and deployment of nuclear weapons to be among the greatest threats to the right to life.[54] Similarly, the CRC Committee repeatedly noted the devastating effects that anti-personnel landmines have had on children and frequently requested States Parties to report on measures they have taken to prevent the production, export and use of landmines.[55]

### 4.3. *Deprivation of Life by State Security Forces*

36. Must the intentional or non-intentional killing of children by the police and other law enforcement personnel be always considered as arbitrary in the sense of Article 6(1) of the CCPR or can we imagine situations in which even the intentional killing of a child might be justified? During the drafting of Article 6 of the CCPR, it was stated that arbitrary deprivation of life contained elements of unlawfulness, injustice, capriciousness and unrea-

---

[53] Human Rights Committee, *o.c.* (note 31), para. 2. *Cf.* M. Nowak, *o.c.* (note 15), p. 125.
[54] Human Rights Committee, *o.c.* (note 15), para. 4.
[55] See R. Hodgkin, P. Newell, *o.c.* (note 28), p. 520.

sonableness.[56] Article 2(2) of the ECHR specifies that deprivation of life shall not be regarded as a violation of the right to life when it results

> 'from the use of force which is no more than absolutely necessary;
>   a. in defence of any person from unlawful violence;
>   b. in order to effect a lawful arrest or to prevent the escape of a person lawfully detained;
>   c. in action lawfully taken for the purpose of quelling a riot or insurrection.'

37. As the examples listed in Article 2(2) of the ECHR, in particular the permission to kill a person in order to effect his or her 'lawful arrest', seem to go rather far, the *European Court of Human Rights* has applied a fairly strict standard on the absolute necessity of using lethal force.[57] Since this standard has led to a violation of Article 2 even in the case of the killing of three adults who were suspected of planning a terrorist attack, it seems to be very difficult for States to argue that the intentional killing of children by security forces was absolutely necessary for any of the purposes cited in Article 2(2) of the ECHR. Taking into account the limited criminal responsibility of children,[58] no case could reasonably be imagined in which the purpose of effecting the lawful arrest of a child or of preventing his or her escape from detention could ever justify the intentional or even non-intentional killing of that child. If children take an active part in internal riots and insurrections, similar standards of special protection of children should apply as in the case of child soldiers taking an active part in international or non-international armed conflicts. As in the case in which a child seriously threatens to kill another person, State security forces might use weapons even against these children. But only in the most extreme cases may such force lead to the intentional or non-intentional killing of children.

### 5. *Obligation to Protect the Right to Life*

38. The obligation to protect refers to the *horizontal effects of human rights*. It obliges States Parties to protect the right to life against undue interference by private Parties. States, therefore, have to take a broad variety of legislative, administrative, judicial and other positive measures to prevent

---

[56] See M. Nowak, *o.c.* (note 15), p. 128.

[57] See *e.g.* Eur Court HR, *McCann, Farrell and Savage v. UK*, judgment of 27 September 1995, Series A, No. 324.

[58] On the respective standards of the CRC, in particular in Articles 37 and 40, see CRC Commentary contributions by W. Schabas and H. Sax (Article 37) and G. Van Bueren (Article 40).

private violence, abuse, exploitation, neglect, traditional and other practices which threaten the life of children. Governments can only be held accountable for such practices if they form a certain pattern or threat that is known or should have been known to the State concerned, and if insufficient action has been taken to prevent such threats and practices. It is primarily up to Governments to decide which type of measures are best suited to prevent specific practices and threats. Taking into account the significance of the right to life as the 'supreme human right' on the one hand, and the particular vulnerability of children on the other, only comprehensive legislative measures in various fields, including criminal law, family law, police and labour law, as well as effective implementation and enforcement of these laws will satisfy the test of *due diligence*, which usually is applied as the relevant standard for the State's obligation to protect. In the following, only a few examples of typical threats to the right to life of children and particularly controversial issues will be discussed.

### 5.1. *Homicide*

39. While Article 6 of the CRC simply refers to the 'inherent right to life' of children, other relevant provisions, such as Article 6(1) of the CCPR, Article 2(1) of the ECHR and Article 4(1) of the ACHR, explicitly provide that this right shall be *protected by law*. First of all, protection by law means that homicide and similar private acts threatening the life of others, including infanticide, must be established in domestic law as *criminal offences punishable by appropriate penalties*. Secondly, the police and other law enforcement bodies have an obligation to take all necessary measures to *prevent homicide* and, in case that such a crime has been committed, to *investigate the crime* with the aim of bringing the perpetrators to justice. The obligation on the part of the police, the public prosecutor and the judiciary to carry out effective criminal investigations and to punish the perpetrators constitutes, therefore, both a procedural obligation deriving from the right to life and an important form of reparation to the victims of such crimes and human rights violations. In cases of gross and systematic violations of the right to life, such as systematic patterns of *summary and arbitrary executions, enforced disappearances and genocide*, whether committed with the active involvement of State actors or not, the criminal responsibility of the individual perpetrators under domestic and international criminal law has become one of the most important means of prevention and reparation.[59]

---

[59] *Cf.* M. Nowak, *o.c.* (note 28), pp. 54–56 and pp. 63–64.

40. A good example of developing the *standard of due diligence* in relation to the prevention of a single case of homicide involving a school child has been provided by the judgment of the *European Court of Human Rights* in *Osman v. UK*.[60] Ahmet Osman was a young boy when his school teacher developed an obsession with him, which led to a serious campaign of harassment, several attacks on his home and an eventual shooting incident where Ahmet was injured, and his father was killed. Although the education authorities and the police were involved from an early stage, the applicant argued that the police had failed to take the necessary measures to safeguard life under Article 2 of the ECHR. The European Court affirmed the principle obligation of States to take preventive operational measures to protect an individual whose life is at risk from the criminal acts of another. A concrete violation of such positive obligation can, however, only be assumed if it is established that the authorities 'knew or ought to have known at the time of the existence of a real and immediate risk to the life of an identified individual . . . from the criminal acts of a third party and that they failed to take measures within the scope of their powers . . . which might have been expected to avoid that risk.'[61] In applying this standard to the case at issue, the European Court denied a violation of the right to life on the ground that there was no decisive stage in the sequence of events leading up to the shooting where the police knew or ought to have known that the lives of the Osman family were at real and immediate risk. But the Court found a violation of the right to a fair trial under Article 6 ECHR on the ground that the British police immunity rule had prevented the applicant from having his claim for negligence against the police authorities determined by the domestic courts.[62] One of the factors to which the Court attached weight in finding a violation of Article 6 of the ECHR was the fact that the case involved the alleged failure to protect the life of a child.

### 5.2. Abortion

41. Whereas Article 4(1) of the ACHR generally protects the right to life 'from the moment of conception',[63] Article 2 of the ECHR, Article 6 of the CCPR and Article 6 of the CRC do not expressly determine the point at which

---

[60] Eur Court HR, *Osman v. United Kingdom*, judgment of 28 October 1998, Reports 1998–VIII, no 95. *Cf. e.g.* U. Kilkelly, *o.c.* (note 37), pp. 143–145.

[61] *Ibid.*, para. 116.

[62] *Ibid.*, paras. 131–154.

[63] See the decision of the Inter-American Commission on Human Rights of 6 March 1981 in the well-known 'Baby Boy' case (no. 2141), in 1981 HRLJ 110.

the protection of the right to life begins. It is, however, clear from the *travaux préparatoires* of Article 6 of the CCPR that the life of the unborn child was not (or not from the moment of conception) to be protected.[64] This restricted understanding of the 'inherent right to life' also applies to Article 6 of the CRC, as the States agreed at a relatively early stage of the CRC drafting process 'not to reopen the discussion concerning the moment at which life begins'.[65] Only the observer for the Holy See strongly emphasized that human life should absolutely be respected and protected from the moment of conception and that a conceived child is entitled to rights.[66] It is, therefore, surprising that States agreed to make a reference in the preamble to a citation from the 1959 Declaration of the Rights of the Child, in which the need for appropriate legal protection, 'before as well as after birth', was stressed.

42. In the recent judgment of *Thi Nho Vo v. France*, the *European Court of Human Rights* confirmed that the issue of when the right to life begins, was a question to be decided at national level.[67] The applicant, a French woman of Vietnamese origin, had been forced to have an abortion after a doctor's mistake when she was six months pregnant. The doctor was first convicted of involuntary homicide but the French Court of Cassation overturned the judgment on the grounds that the foetus had not yet been a human being, entitled to the protection of criminal law. The judgment of the European Court means, in effect, that the obligation of States under Article 2 of the ECHR to protect the right to life against private interference by criminal law does not apply to the unborn child.

43. Since also the definition of the child in Article 1 of the CRC deliberately leaves open the starting point of childhood, it is left to the States Parties to decide for themselves the conflicting rights and interests involved in issues such as abortion and family planning.[68] Some States Parties entered specific *declarations and reservations* in this respect.[69] The People's Republic of China, *e.g.*, reserved its one child family planning policy as laid down in Article 25 of the Constitution and Article 2 of the Law of Minor Children.

---

[64] See M. Nowak, *o.c.* (note 15), pp. 153–154.

[65] See *supra*, III.1. and S. Detrick, *o.c.* (note 6), p. 121. See also S. Detrick, *o.c.* (note 28), pp. 133–134.

[66] See S. Detrick, *o.c.* (note 6), p. 122.

[67] Eur Court HR, *Thi Nho Vo v.* France, judgment by the Grand Chamber of 8 July 2004.

[68] See R. Hodgkin, P. Newell, *o.c.* (note 28), p. 97.

[69] For the text of these declarations and reservations see UN Doc. CRC/C/2/Rev. 5. See also R. Hodgkin, P. Newell, *o.c.* (note 28), pp. 3–4.

France and Tunisia declared that Article 6 of the CRC cannot be interpreted as constituting any obstacle to the implementation of the provisions of their respective legislation relating to the voluntary interruption of pregnancy. Luxembourg made a similar declaration in respect of its legislation concerning sex information, the prevention of back-street abortion and the regulation of pregnancy termination. The United Kingdom declared that it interprets the CRC as applicable only following a life birth. Argentina, in contrast, declared that Article 1 of the CRC must be interpreted to the effect that a child means every human being from the moment of conception up to the age of 18.

44. The *CRC Committee* has repeatedly suggested that reservations to preserve State laws on abortion and family planning are unnecessary in light of the fact that the CRC deliberately leaves these issues within the individual States' discretion. It, *e.g.*, explicitly encouraged *China* to withdraw its reservation. At the same time, the Committee has commented adversely on high rates of abortion and on the use of abortion as a method of family planning, and it has encouraged States, such as the Russian Federation, Romania and Belarus, to reduce the high number of abortions.[70] But the Committee has also expressed concern at 'clandestine' abortions.[71] This is in line with a General Comment on the equality between men and women, in which the *Human Rights Committee* had urged States to provide information on any measures to help women prevent unwanted pregnancies, 'and to ensure that they do not have to undergo life-threatening clandestine abortions'.[72] Similarly, the *CEDAW Committee*, in a General Recommendation on women and health, had asked States to amend legislation criminalizing abortion in order to 'withdraw punitive measures imposed on women who undergo abortion'.[73]

45. With the advance of pre-natal diagnostic techniques, the possibilities for misusing this medical technology for the purpose of *selective and discriminatory abortions* increased. Some States have introduced laws on abortion that permit termination of pregnancy at a later stage when tests have indicated that the foetus has a disabling impairment. In its recommenda-

---

[70] See *ibid.*, pp. 97–98.
[71] See *e.g.* CRC Committee, *Concluding Observations Nicaragua* (UN Doc. CRC/C/15/Add. 36). See also R. Hodgkin, P. Newell, *o.c.* (note 28), p. 98.
[72] Human Rights Committee, *General Comment No. 28: The quality of rights between men and women* (UN Doc. HRI/GEN/Rev.7), para. 10.
[73] CEDAW Committee, *General Recommendation No. 24: Women and Health* (UN Doc. HRI/GEN/Rev. 7), para. 31 (c).

tions adopted following the 1997 General Discussion on the *rights of children with disabilities*, the CRC Committee adopted a fairly far-reaching position on this highly sensitive and controversial question when it urged States to review and amend legislation which 'denies disabled children an equal right to life, survival and development, including—in those States which allow abortion—discriminatory laws on abortion affecting disabled children, and discriminatory access to health services'.[74]

46.  Less controversial seem to be problems arising from modern techniques of *pre-natal sex selection*. In its comprehensive second periodic report of 2001, the Government of *India* has devoted a considerable part of its chapter on the right to life to this problem:[75]

> 'The negative bias against women has taken an alarming dimension recently with the utilisation of the amniocentesis test for detecting the sex of the foetus, followed by selective abortion of the foetus if detected to be female. Apart from the considerable risks to the foetus and the woman, the utilisation of pre-natal diagnostic techniques for selective abortion of female foetuses perpetuates the negative social worth of women . . . The sharp decline in female sex ratios over the years suggests that female infanticide and foeticide might be largely responsible for this phenomenon rather than general neglect of the girl child. The sex ratio is a sensitive indicator of the status of women in any society and the decline in the sex ratio in some States is a great cause for concern.'

Already during the examination of the initial report, the CRC Committee had responded to this sensitive question by encouraging the Government of India to 'undertake studies to determine the socio-cultural factors which lead to practices such as female infanticide and selective abortions, and to develop strategies to address them'.[76]

47.  One might conclude from this short survey on the controversial issue of abortion that the CRC Committee, similar to the Human Rights Committee and the European Court of Human Rights, starts from the assumption, which also derives from the *travaux préparatoires*, that the obligation of States to protect the right to life by means of criminal law does not apply to the unborn child and that States Parties are, therefore, free to decide whether and to what extent they wish to prohibit abortions, provided, of course,

---

[74] CRC Committee, *General Discussion on the Rights of Children with Disabilities* (UN Doc. CRC/C/66), Annex V. See also R. Hodgkin, P. Newell, *o.c.* (note 28), p. 98.
[75] CRC Committee, *Concludine Observations: India* (UN Doc. CRC/C93/Add. 5, 2003), paras. 251–252.
[76] CRC Committee, *Concludine Observations: India* (UN Doc. CRC/C/15/Add. 115, 2000), para. 49.

that they do not violate the human rights of the mother, such as the rights to privacy, equality and reproductive health. On the other hand, various critical comments and recommendations of the CRC Committee on the frequent recourse to abortion as a method of family planning and on the sensitive issue of selective and discriminatory abortions in the context of the right to life show that the Committee is not fully consistent on its interpretation of Article 6 of the CRC in this respect. As the UNICEF Implementation Handbook for the CRC observes, these sensitive human rights issues become more and more complex as medical technology advances, and pose a greater number of ethical dilemmas and possible conflicts between the rights of the child and his or her mother.[77]

### 5.3. *Infanticide*

48. While the application of Article 6 of the CRC to the unborn child remains controversial, States are, of course, obliged to protect children against infanticide, and in particular against practices based on discriminatory grounds, such as sex and disability. As we just discussed in relation to the situation in India, the sex ratio is a sensitive indicator of the status of women in a given society. If boys are valued economically and socially above girls, unequal population figures and, even more alarmingly, a decline in the sex ratio of girls, indicate that infanticide may still be widespread.[78] Many legal systems recognize the particular crime of infanticide as a distinctly defined form of homicide with reduced penalties. Although these laws might be well-intended as to provide a special defence for mothers suffering psychological trauma as a result of the process of birth, they 'appear to discriminate against children as victims of homicide'.[79] In addition, these laws might have the effect of indirect discrimination against the most vulnerable groups of children, such as the girl-child, children with disabilities, minority children or children born as a result of rape, enforced pregnancy and motherhood or a policy of 'ethnic cleansing'.[80]

49. The *CRC Committee* expressed its concern at high rates of infanticide in relation to various countries. In its Concluding Observations on Benin, *e.g.*,

---

[77] R. Hodgkin, P. Newell, *o.c.* (note 28), p. 98.
[78] *Cf.* R. Hodgkin, P. Newell, *o.c.* (note 28), pp. 100–102.
[79] *Ibid.*, p. 102.
[80] *Cf. e.g.* J. Daniel, "No Man's Child—The War Rape Orphans", in European Master's Degree in Human Rights and Democratisation (EMA), Awarded Theses of the Academic Year 2002/2003 (Venice, Marsilio Editori, 2004), pp. 11–96.

the Committee noted that infanticide continued to be practised, particularly in rural communities and on infants with disabilities. It recommended that the Government of Benin seek to 'fully implement article 6 of the Convention and take measures, including those of a legal nature, to prevent and discourage infanticide and protect infants and guarantee their right to life, survival and development'.[81] With respect to China, the Committee was alarmed at the distorted gender ratio as a consequence of the one child family planning policy. It urged the Government of China to 'take further action for the maintenance of strong and comprehensive measures to combat the abandonment and infanticide of girls as well as the trafficking, sale and kidnapping or abduction of girls'.[82]

### 5.4. *Harmful Traditional Practices*

50. According to Article 24(3) of the CRC, States Parties 'shall take all effective and appropriate measures with a view to abolishing traditional practices prejudicial to the health of children'.[83] Article 21 of the *African Charter on the Rights and Welfare of the Child* of 1990 even devotes a separate provision to the protection against harmful social and cultural practices. Article 21(1) of the Charter reads as follows:

> 'States Parties to the present Charter shall take all appropriate measures to eliminate harmful social and cultural practices affecting the welfare, dignity, normal growth and development of the child and in particular:
> a) those customs and practices prejudicial to the health or life of the child; and
> b) those customs and practices discriminatory to the child on the grounds of sex or other status.'

51. In addition to being discriminatory and endangering the right to health, many traditional practices in various societies amount to violations or serious threats to the right to life of children, and in particular the girl child. A typical example of such practices, which constitutes in fact a special type of infanticide or homicide exempted from normal criminal responsibility, are the so-called '*honour killings*'. In the Islamic Republic of Iran, *e.g.*, a special provision of the Penal Law provided that a man who kills his own child or his son's child is subject only to discretionary punishment and the payment

---

[81] CRC Committee, *Concluding Observations: Benin* (UN Doc. CRC/C/15/Add. 106, 1999), para. 16.
[82] CRC Committee, *Concluding Observations: China* (UN Doc. CRC/C/15/Add. 56, 1996), para. 36.
[83] On traditional practices harmful to the right to health. See also G. Van Bueren, *o.c.* (note 29), pp. 307–310.

of blood money. In its Concluding Observations, the CRC Committee urged the Iranian Government to 'take all necessary measures to ensure that there is no discriminatory treatment for such crimes and ensure prompt and thorough investigation and prosecutions'.[84] Most notorious are the provisions in the Penal Code of *Jordan* which condone crimes perpetrated in the name of honour. In its Concluding Observations, the Committee, in line with other UN bodies,[85] urged the Jordanian Government to take 'all necessary measures to ensure that there is no discriminatory treatment for crimes of honour and that they are promptly and thoroughly investigated and prosecuted. In addition, the Committee recommends to the State Party to undertake awareness-raising activities demonstrating that such practices are socially and morally unacceptable'.[86]

52. In spring 2003, the CRC Committee adopted a *General Comment on 'Adolescent health and development* in the context of the Convention on the Rights of the Child' which contains the following paragraph on traditional practices:[87]

> 'In light of articles 3, 6, 12, 19 and 24(3) of the Convention, States parties should take all effective measures to eliminate all acts and activities which threaten the right to life of adolescents, including honour killings. The Committee strongly urges States parties to develop and implement awareness-raising campaigns, education programmes and legislation aimed at changing prevailing attitudes, and address gender roles and stereotypes that contribute to harmful traditional practices. Further, States parties should facilitate the establishment of multidisciplinary information and advice centres regarding the harmful aspects of some traditional practices, including early marriage and female genital mutilation.'

In January 2003, the Committee had already adopted a *General Comment on 'HIV/AIDS* and the rights of the child', in which it stressed that 'the female child is often subject to harmful traditional practices, such as early and/or forced marriage, which violate her rights and make her more vulnerable to

---

[84] CRC Committee, *Concluding Observations: Iran* (UN Doc. CRC/C/15/Add. 123, 2000), para. 28.
[85] *Cf. e.g.* the recommendations of the Special Rapporteur on extrajudicial, summary and arbitrary executions, UN Doc. E/CN.4/2000/3; Commission on Human Rights, resolutions 2000/31 and 45.
[86] CRC Committee, *Concluding Observations: Jordan* (UN Doc. CRC/C/15/Add. 125, 2000), para. 36.
[87] CRC Committee, *General Comment No. 4: Adolescent health and development in the context of the Convention on the Rights of the Child* (UN Doc. CRC/GC/2003/4), para. 24.

HIV infection, including because such practices often interrupt access to education and information'.[88]

53. An *early age of marriage for girls* not only raises an issue of discrimination under Article 2 of the CRC but also threatens the rights of both the child-mother and the newly born child to life and to maximum survival and development under Article 6.[89] According to the Platform of Action of the Fourth World Conference on Women, held in Beijing in 1995, 'more than 15 million girls aged 15 to 19 give birth each year. Motherhood at a very young age entails complications during pregnancy and delivery and a risk of maternal death that is much greater than average. The children of young mothers have higher levels of morbidity and mortality'.[90] In its Concluding Observations on Nicaragua (1995), *e.g.*, the CRC Committee expressed the view that 'the early and lower marriageable age for girls as compared with boys raises serious questions as to their compatibility with the principles and provisions of the Convention, in particular those laid down in its articles 2, 3 and 6'.[91] On the basis of the general principles of the CRC, including the right to life, the Committee, therefore, recommended to various Governments to adopt the same age of marriage for girls and boys.[92] Most advanced in this regard seems to be Article 21(2) of the *African Charter on the Rights and Welfare of the Child*:

> 'Child marriage and the betrothal of girls and boys shall be prohibited and effective action, including legislation, shall be taken to specify the minimum age of marriage to be eighteen years and make registration of all marriages in an official registry compulsory.'[93]

54. One of the most widespread and harmful traditional practices is *female genital mutilation* (FGM). The World Health Organization estimates that over 100 million girls and women have suffered FGM, of whom some 15 million

---

[88] CRC Committee, *General Comment No. 3: HIV/AIDS and the rights of the child* (UN Doc. CRC/GC/2003/3), para. 11.

[89] *Cf.* R. Hodgkin, P. Newell, *o.c.* (note 28), p. 98.

[90] UN Doc. A/CONF.177/20/Rev. 1, para. 268.

[91] CRC Committee, *Concluding Observations: Nicaragua* (UN Doc. CRC/C/15/Add. 36, 1995), para. 13. See also L. Holmström, *o.c.* (note 26), p. 345.

[92] *Cf. e.g.* CRC Committee, *Concluding Observations: Ukraine* (UN Doc. CRC/C/15/Add. 42, 1995), para. 17. See also L. Holmström, *supra* (note 26), p. 507.

[93] This provision is based on Article 16(2) of the CEDAW which provides that the betrothal and marriage of a child shall have no legal effect. At the time of the adoption of the CEDAW in 1979, the term 'child' did, however, not yet include adolescents, and States Parties were only required to specify a minimum age for marriage.

have been infibulated.[94] It is common practice in more than half of all African States. Approximately 75% of all cases are found in Nigeria, Ethiopia, Egypt, Sudan and Kenya. In some States, such as Djibouti, Somalia, Eritrea, Ethiopia, Sierra Leone and Sudan, more than 80% of girls have been circumcised. Article 2(a) of the *UN Declaration on the Elimination of Violence against Women* of 1993 lists FGM as an explicit example of traditional practices harmful to women, and there can no longer be any doubt that FGM figures prominently among those traditional practices that should urgently be eliminated by States in accordance with the provisions of Article 24(3) of the CRC and Article 21(1) of the African Charter cited above. Already in 1986, the report of the Commission on Human Rights Working Group on Traditional Practices affecting the health of Women and Children had recommended the elimination of FGM[95] and, on the basis of a resolution of the Commission of 1987, the Sub-Commission has appointed a Special Rapporteur on this issue.[96] In 1994, the Sub-Commission adopted a 'Plan of Action for the Elimination of Harmful Traditional Practices affecting the Health of Women and Children', which called on States to put an end to harmful traditional practices, particularly female circumcision.[97] Nevertheless, the issue of FGM remains a 'cultural minefield'.[98]

55.   In its General Guidelines for periodic reports of 1996, the *CRC Committee* requested States Parties to provide information on the measures adopted with a view to abolishing traditional practices prejudicial to the health of children, as for example, genital mutilation and forced marriage.[99] In its concluding observations on the reports of various States Parties, the Committee repeatedly urged Governments to take stronger action against FGM. For example, it requested the Government of Sudan as well as religious and community leaders 'to take an active role in supporting efforts to eliminate the practice of female genital mutilation'.[100]

---

[94]  See *e.g.* WHO, Factsheet Nr. 241, June 2000 (http://www.who.int/); UNICEF, Factsheet: FGM (http://www.unicef.org/); G. Van Bueren, *o.c.* (note 29), pp. 307–310; S. Detrick, *o.c.* (note 28), pp. 414–419.

[95]  UN Doc. E/CN.4/1986/42.

[96]  Commission resolutions 1987/57 and 1988/57. See the reports of the Special Rapporteur in UN Docs. E/CN.4/Sub.2/1989/42 and E/CN.4/Sub.2/1996/6.

[97]  UN Doc. E/CN.4/Sub.2/1994/10/Add.1. See also CEDAW-Committee, *General Recommendation No. 14: Female Circumcision* (UN Doc. A/45/38), para. 438.

[98]  G. Van Bueren, *o.c.* (note 29), p. 309.

[99]  CRC Committee, *General Guidelines regarding the form and the contents of periodic reports* (UN Doc. CRC/C/58), para. 97.

[100]  CRC Committee, *Concluding Observations: Sudan* (UN Doc. CRC/C/15/Add. 10), para. 22; see also R. Hodgkin, P. Newell, *o.c.* (note 28), p. 352.

### 5.5. *Other Forms of Violence, Abuse and Exploitation Endangering the Right to Life*

56. Children are exposed to many forms of private violence, abuse and exploitation which cause serious risks to their right to life and, therefore, need to be addressed by appropriate legislative, administrative, judicial and other positive measures by States Parties. Since the CRC contains a comprehensive list of provisions which establish specific obligations of States Parties to protect children against various forms of violence, abuse and exploitation, we will confine ourselves to identifying these provisions and refer the reader to the respective commentaries below:

– Article 19: State obligation to protect the child from all forms of physical or mental violence, injury or abuse, neglect or negligent treatment, maltreatment or exploitation, including sexual abuse, while in the care of parent(s), legal guardian(s) or any other person who has the care of the child;
– Article 32: Right of the child to be protected from economic exploitation and from performing any work that is likely to be hazardous or to interfere with the child's education, or to be harmful to the child's health or physical, mental, spiritual, moral or social development;
– Article 33: State obligation to protect children from the illicit use of narcotic drugs and psychotropic substances and to prevent the use of children in the illicit production and trafficking of such substances;
– Article 34: State obligation to protect children from all forms of sexual exploitation and sexual abuse, including child prostitution and child pornography;
– Article 35: State obligation to prevent the abduction of, the sale of or traffic in children for any purpose or in any form;
– Article 36: State obligation to protect children against all other forms of exploitation prejudicial to any aspects of the child's welfare.

57. In addition, the UN General Assembly adopted an *Optional Protocol to the CRC on the sale of children, child prostitution and child pornography* in May 2000, which entered into force in January 2002.[101] The OP defines these three types of child abuse and exploitation and establishes precise obligations of States Parties to take criminal action against child traffickers and persons involved in child prostitution and child pornography. Finally, the ILO General Conference in 1999 adopted the *Worst Forms of Child Labour Convention*, which establishes, as a matter of urgency, an obligation of States Parties to secure the prohibition and elimination of the following worst forms of labour for all children under the age of 18:[102]

---

[101] GA Res. 54/263 of 25 May 2000; entry into force on 18 January 2002.
[102] Article 3 of ILO Convention No. 182 of 17 June 1999; entry into force on 19 November 2000.

- All forms of slavery or practices similar to slavery, such as the sale and trafficking of children, debt bondage and serfdom and forced or compulsory
labour, including forced or compulsory recruitment of children for use in
armed forces;
- The use, procuring or offering of a child for prostitution, for the production of pornography or for pornographic performances;
- The use, procuring or offering of a child for illicit activities, in particular
for the production and trafficking of drugs;
- Work which, by its nature or the circumstances in which it is carried out,
is likely to harm the health, safety or morals of children.

### 6. Obligation to Fulfil the Right to Life

58.  The *travaux préparatoires* of Article 6 clearly show the interdependence
of both paragraphs.[103] The 1988 proposal of India to include a separate right
to survival was meant to protect children from dying of preventable diseases, and, according to UNICEF and the WHO, the concept of survival
included growth monitoring, oral rehydration and disease control, breast-
feeding, immunization, child spacing, food and female literacy. Thus, survival was closely linked to the healthy development of children in a
comprehensive sense. In the opinion of the drafters of Article 6, para. 1 represented the traditional obligations of States to respect the life of children
through non-interference, whereas para. 2 entailed positive obligations of
States to ensure the survival and development of the child by comprehensive measures of protection and fulfilment. However, the underlying assumption that the right to life merely referred to negative State obligations did
not correspond anymore to the interpretation of civil and political rights
at that time. Already in 1982 had the *Human Rights Committee*, in its first
General Comment on the right to life in Article 6 of the CCPR, called upon
States Parties 'to take all possible measures to reduce infant mortality and
to increase life expectancy, especially in adopting measures to eliminate
malnutrition and epidemics'.[104] While some commentators on Article 6 of
the CCPR still followed the traditional liberal approach of interpretation,[105]
others argued already at that time that States have a strict international
responsibility under Article 6 of the CCPR to create satisfactory conditions

---

[103] See *supra*, III.1.
[104] Human Rights Committee, *o.c.* (note 15), para. 4.
[105] *Cf. e.g.* Y. Dinstein, 'The Right to Life, Physical Integrity and Liberty', in Louis Henkin
(ed.), *The International Bill of Rights—The Covenant on Civil and Political Rights* (New York, Colombia
University Press, 1981), p. 114 *et seq.*; see also the criticism by G. Van Bueren, *o.c.* (note 29),
p. 302.

for survival.[106] In any case, both the wording and the drafting history of Article 6 of the CRC leave no doubt that the right to life, survival and development obliges States Parties to adopt a holistic approach to the child's development and to take comprehensive positive measures to fulfil, to the maximum extent possible, the survival and healthy development of the child. This general principle in Article 6 is further defined in a number of additional provisions of the CRC relating to the rights of the child to health, education, rest, leisure and play etc.

### 6.1. *The Role of the Parents*

59. According to Article 18(1) of the CRC, parents, or, as the case may be, legal guardians, 'have the primary responsibility for the upbringing and development of the child. The best interests of the child will be their basic concern'. States Parties shall recognize the principle that *both* parents have common responsibilities for the upbringing and development of the child and, pursuant to Article 5, shall respect the responsibilities, rights and duties of parents to provide, in a manner consistent with the *evolving capacities of the child*, appropriate direction and guidance in the exercise by the child of the rights recognized in the CRC. The concept of the evolving capacities must be interpreted in a dynamic sense, and pursuant to the general principle in Article 12, the views of the child must be respected and given due weight in accordance with the age and maturity of the child. The Convention is thus based on the principle of recognizing the *family as the 'natural and fundamental group unit of society'*[107] and the 'natural environment for the growth and well-being of all its members and particularly children'.[108] In the preamble of the CRC, States Parties explicitly recognize that 'the child, for the full and harmonious development of his or her personality, should grow up in a family environment, in an atmosphere of happiness, love and understanding'.[109] Consequently, States Parties shall ensure, save in truly exceptional circumstances, such as serious violence, abuse and neglect of children, that a child shall not be separated from his or her parents, that separated children maintain personal relations and direct contact with both parents, and that the right to family reunification shall be respected in the case of children who live in different countries than their parents.[110]

---

[106] B. Ramacharan, 'The Right to Life', *NILR* 1983, pp. 297, 298, 307.
[107] *Cf.* Article 23 of the CCPR, Article 10 of the CESCR.
[108] 4th preambular paragraph of the CRC.
[109] 5th preambular paragraph of the CRC.
[110] See Articles 9 and 10 of the CRC. See also the right of children under Article 7(1) of the CRC to 'be cared for by his or her parents'.

60. For the purpose of guaranteeing and promoting the rights of the child, States Parties, pursuant to Article 18(2) of the CRC, shall render appropriate *assistance to parents* and legal guardians in the performance of their child-rearing responsibilities and shall ensure the development of institutions, facilities, and services for the care of children. This is in line with the general principle of the subsidiary responsibility of States Parties to ensure protection and care, as stipulated in Article 3(2) of the CRC. In particular, children of working parents have the right to benefit from child-care services. Should children, for whatever reason, be temporarily or permanently deprived of their family environment, then Article 20 entitles them to 'special protection and assistance provided by the State', such as foster placement, adoption or, if necessary, placement in a suitable institution for the care of children. Special protection by the State shall also be provided to children with disabilities, refugee and minority children in accordance with Articles 22, 23 and 30 of the CRC.

61. The Convention, taken as a whole, is based on the philosophy that the parents bear the primary responsibility for ensuring the survival, development and upbringing of their children in accordance with their evolving capacities. States Parties have the obligation to fulfil the right to life, survival and development, first of all, by *respecting and facilitating the responsibility of parents* by all appropriate means, such as financial assistance, the establishment and development of child-care services and facilities etc. The more vulnerable children become (orphans, children separated from their parents, internally displaced and refugee children, children with disabilities, children of poor parents etc.) the more important the respective State obligation to fulfil becomes. In addition to these specific duties to assist parents and to take care of children, States also have a more general obligation to take measures of creating an environment conducive to the best possible survival and healthy development of children. In the following, some of the most important elements of this obligation to fulfil will be dealt with in light of the respective practice of the CRC Committee.

### 6.2. Registration of Children

62. Article 7 of the CRC provides that the child 'shall be registered immediately after birth and shall have the right from birth to a name, the right to acquire a nationality and, as far as possible, the right to know and be cared for by his or her parents'. According to UNICEF statistics, in the year 2000, over 50 million babies were not registered, *i.e.* 41% of births world-

wide. In Sub-Saharan Africa, even 71% of all newly born babies were not registered.[111] Children who are not registered at birth are denied their identity, a recognized name and a nationality. They are not recognized as a 'person before the law' in the sense of Article 16 of the CCPR, and their death, by infanticide, disease or malnutrition, might even go unnoticed by the respective State authorities. In other words, the *birth registration of babies* is a very important pre-condition for the right to life, survival and development of children.

63.  The same holds true for the *registration of deaths*. In its General Guidelines for periodic reports, the CRC Committee requested States Parties to provide information 'on the measures taken to ensure the registration of the deaths of children, the causes of death and, where appropriate, investigation and reporting on such deaths'.[112] It goes without saying that establishing proper procedures for registering all deaths and for independently investigating the causes of child deaths reduces the possibility of cover-up, reveals the extent of violence, abuse and neglect of children, enables the authorities, where appropriate, to bring the perpetrators of violence and infanticide to justice, and facilitates preventive strategies, such as support for parents, education, the reduction of suicides and accident prevention.[113]

### 6.3. *Suicide*

64.  In its examination of State reports, the CRC Committee has repeatedly expressed concern at high, and in some countries, increasing rates of suicide among children, and in particular male adolescents.[114] This concern is so strong that the Committee, in its General Guidelines for periodic reports, urged States Parties to provide information on 'the measures adopted to prevent children's suicide and monitor its incidence and . . . to provide relevant disaggregated data, including on the number of suicides among children'.[115] Often, higher rates of suicide occur among discriminated or particularly vulnerable groups of children. For example, in *Canada*, where the average of suicides among *indigenous youths* seemed to have been five

---

[111]  See UNICEF, *o.c.* (note 1), p. 76.
[112]  CRC Committee, *o.c.* (note 99), para. 41.
[113]  *Cf.* R. Hodgkin and P. Newell, *o.c.* (note 28), p. 103.
[114]  *Cf.* the Concluding Observations on various States, primarily in the industrialized world, in R. Hodgkin and P. Newell, *o.c.* (note 28), p. 102.
[115]  CRC Committee, *o.c.* (note 99), para. 41.

times higher than the average among non-Indians, the Committee recommended that 'research should be developed on the problems relating to the growing rate of infant mortality and suicide among children within aboriginal communities'.[116]

### 6.4. *Traffic Accidents and Street Violence*

65. Another common cause of preventable death, affecting children in particular, is traffic accidents.[117] For example, the CRC Committee requested the Government of *Jordan*, due to the high incidence of traffic accidents, which claim the lives of children, to 'strengthen and continue efforts to raise awareness about and undertake public information campaigns in relation to accident prevention'.[118]

66. In its General Guidelines for periodic reports, the CRC Committee requested States Parties to provide information on the measures taken to prevent certain risks to which adolescents may be particularly exposed, for example street violence.[119] It goes without saying that *street children*, which constitute a considerable group of adolescents in many countries of the South, including Brazil and Colombia, are exposed to a much higher risk of violence, exploitation, abuse, enforced disappearance and similar threats to their right to life, than children who grow up in a protected family environment. With respect to *Nepal*, for example, the CRC Committee has urged the Government that 'firm measures be taken to ensure the right of survival of all children in Nepal, including those who live and/or work in the streets'.[120]

### 6.5. *Infant and Child Mortality*

67. The infant and child mortality rates constitute the most important indicators for monitoring the implementation of the State obligation to fulfil the right of children to life and survival. The *infant mortality rate* indicates the probability of dying between birth and exactly one year of age expressed by 1,000 live births. The *child or under 5—five mortality rate* indicates the probability of dying between birth and exactly five years of age expressed per

---

[116] CRC Committee, *Concluding Observations: Canada* (UN Doc. CRC/C/15/Add. 37, 1995), para. 26.

[117] *Cf.* R. Hodgkin and P. Newell, *o.c.* (note 28), p. 103.

[118] CRC Committee, *Concluding Observation: Jordan* (UN Doc. CRC/C/15/Add. 125, 2000), para. 38.

[119] CRC Committee, *o.c.* (note 99), para. 41.

[120] CRC Committee, *Concluding Observations: Nepal* (UN Doc. CRC/C/15/Add. 57, 1996), para. 35.

1,000 births. According to UN statistics, worldwide 57 out of 1,000 babies have died in 2001 before reaching their first birthday, and 82 out of 1,000 children have died before reaching the age of five.[121] As compared to 1960, when the respective figures were as high as 126 and 197, respectively, the overall reduction of these mortality rates can be considered as a success. But the discrepancies between rich and poor countries widened during the same 40 years. While the gap between industrialized and least developed countries regarding the infant mortality rate amounted in 1960 to 31:170 (less than 6 times), it amounted in 2001 to 5:100 (20 times as high). Whereas in *Sweden* only three children out of 1,000 died before the age of five in 2001, the infant and child mortality rate in *Sierra Leone* amounted to 182 and 316, respectively.

68. Similarly, while the *life expectancy at birth, i.e.* the number of years new-born children would live if subject to the mortality risks prevailing for the cross-section of population at the time of their birth, has reached 80 in Sweden and 79 in Australia, Belgium, Canada, France, Iceland, Israel, Italy, Norway, Spain, and Switzerland, the children born in 2001 in Botswana and Mozambique (39), Malawi, Rwanda and Sierra Leone (40), Burundi (41), Djibouti, Swaziland and Zambia (42), Afghanistan and Zimbabwe (43) enjoy on average only half a life expectancy as compared to children born in the most highly developed countries of our world.[122] There are, of course, many reasons to explain these figures. In the countries of Southern Africa mentioned above, *HIV/AIDS* seems to be a major reason for the low life expectancy. In Afghanistan, Sierra Leone, Rwanda, Burundi and Djibouti *armed conflicts* and *ethnic violence* might play a significant role, but the *lack of adequate sanitation and health services* caused by *extreme poverty* is, of course, the main reason for the high infant and child mortality rates in these countries.

69. The diseases most commonly associated with infant and child mortality include pneumonia, diarrhoea and immunisable diseases,[123] *i.e.* most deaths of children in poor and developing countries are in fact preventable. According to WHO figures,[124] in 1990 some 4,3 million children under 5 years

---

[121] See UNICEF, *o.c.* (note 1), pp. 84–87.

[122] *Ibid.*

[123] *Cf.* G. Van Bueren, *o.c.* (note 29), p. 304; D. Parker and C. Sepúlveda, 'Children's right to survival and healthy development', in J.R. Himes (ed.), *Implementing the Convention on the Rights of the Child—Resource Mobilization in Low-Income Countries* (The Hague/London/Boston, Martinus Nijhoff Publishers, 1995), pp. 79–81.

[124] For the following see World Health Organization, *Implementation of the Global Strategy for Health for All by the Year 2000* (Geneva, WHO, 1993), p. 107; D. Parker and C. Sepúlveda, *o.c.*

of age (one third of the total) died from pneumonia and other *acute respi-ratory infections* (ARI), such as measles and pertussis. *Pneumonia*, basically of bacterial origin in children, constituted the single-largest cause of child mortality, chiefly because parents either do not know when to seek treat-ment, or because they do not complete treatment. *Neonatal and perinatal deaths* from different causes (birth asphyxia, neonatal tetanus, congenital anomalies, birth trauma, prematurity, neonatal sepsis and meningitis) in 1990 formed the second largest grouping, accounting for 3.8 million deaths, or 30 per cent of the total. These were followed by *diarrhoea*-related deaths (3.2 million, or one fourth of the total), and *vaccine-preventable deaths* (such as neonatal tetanus, measles, tuberculosis, pertussis), which accounted for 2.1 million deaths (16 per cent of the total). Measles was responsible for nearly two thirds (880.000) of these latter deaths.

70. In the meantime, *HIV/AIDS* has become another major source of deaths for both adults and children. In Sub-Saharan Africa, the adult HIV preva-lence rate amounts to 8.6 per cent, in some countries in Southern Africa, such as Botswana, Lesotho and Swaziland, it has reached already more than 30 per cent.[125] Initially children were considered to be only marginally affected by this epidemic. However, the international community has dis-covered that, unfortunately, children are at the heart of the problem.[126] In most parts of the world, the majority of new infections are among young people between the ages of 15 and 24, sometimes younger. The vast major-ity of infected women and girls do not know that they are infected and may unknowingly infect their children. According to UNICEF statistics of 2003, some 14 million children in the world under 15 years of age have lost one or both parents to AIDS.[127]

71. Young children are in particular need to be protected against these dis-eases as they are more vulnerable to infectious and birth related diseases and, of course, cannot take care of themselves. If their health needs and requirements are not satisfied during early childhood, this will have seri-ous effects on their future physical and mental survival, development and life. From an ethical and political point of view, it is simply unacceptable that 35,000 children should die each day, most of them in poor countries

(note 123), pp. 79–81. See also the report of the UNSG and UNICEF to the World Summit of Children in May 2002: http://www. unicef.org/specialsession/about/sg-report.htm.
[125] See UNICEF, *o.c.* (note 1), pp. 92–95.
[126] See CRC Committee, *o.c.* (note 88).
[127] UNICEF, *o.c.* (note 1), p. 78.

and from a preventable cause.[128] The *reduction of child mortality* by various means, such as education, immunisation, oral rehydration therapy (ORT) and other health measures for the prevention of child diseases, has, therefore, long been a priority of development policies and programmes. In the *Millennium Development Goals* of 2000, UN Member States have pledged to reduce, by the year 2015, the child mortality rate by two-thirds, the maternal mortality ratio by three-quarters, and to combat HIV/AIDS, malaria and other major diseases.

72. But the CRC goes beyond mere moral responsibilities and political pledges. It establishes *legal rights of children* to the 'highest attainable standard of health', to a 'standard of living adequate for the child's physical, mental, spiritual, moral and social development', to nutrition, clothing, housing, education and social security, just to name some of the most important human rights of children which are directly linked to the umbrella right of the child to life, survival and development. These human rights of children entail *legal claims and entitlements with corresponding legal obligations* of their parents, the society they live in, States Parties to the CRC as well as the international community in a rapidly globalizing society. Since all these rights will be dealt with in detail in other chapters of this Commentary, only the most fundamental aspects of these rights and corresponding State obligations will be addressed in the following in order to illustrate what the CRC Committee means when it designed the right to life, survival and development as one of the four general principles of the Convention.

### 6.6. *Obligation to Fulfil the Healthy Development of the Child*

73. Article 24 of the CRC is most directly related to the right to life and can be regarded as a legal definition of some of the most fundamental State obligations deriving from the right of children to survival and development.[129] Pursuant to Article 24(1), States Parties recognize 'the *right of the child to the enjoyment of the highest attainable standard of health* and to facilities for the treatment of illness and rehabilitation of health'. States Parties shall 'strive to ensure that no child is deprived of his or her right of access to such health care services'.

---

[128] D. Parker and C. Sepúlveda, *o.c.* (note 123), pp. 72–73.

[129] In its General Guidelines for periodic reports (CRC Committee, *o.c.* (note 99), para. 93), the CRC Committee combines the measures which States have to take in relation to both Articles 6 and 24 of the CRC. In the literature on the CRC, the right to life in Article 6 and the right to health in Article 24 are usually treated together: see, *e.g.*, G. Van Bueren, *o.c.* (note 29), pp. 293–327; D. Parker and C. Sepúlveda, *o.c.* (note 123), pp. 69–106.

74. In Article 24(2), some of the most important States' *obligations to fulfil the right to health* are listed, such as

- To diminish infant and child mortality;
- To ensure the provision of necessary medical assistance and health care to all children with emphasis on the development of primary health care;
- To combat disease and malnutrition, including within the framework of primary health care, through, *inter alia*, the application of readily available technology and through the provision of adequate nutritious foods and clean drinking-water, taking into consideration the dangers and risks of environmental pollution;
- To ensure appropriate pre-natal and post-natal health care for mothers;
- To ensure that all segments of society, in particular parents and children, are informed, have access to education and are supported in the use of basic knowledge of child health and nutrition, the advantages of breast-feeding, hygiene and environmental sanitation and the prevention of accidents;
- To develop preventive health care, guidance for parents and family planning education and services.

75. In its General Guidelines for periodic reports, the *CRC Committee* further defined the obligations of States Parties to report on the implementation of these obligations, on the progress achieved and the difficulties encountered. In particular, the Committee requires States to identify relevant targets, indicators and benchmarks and to provide relevant disaggregated data, including by gender, age, region, rural/urban area, ethnic and social origin.[130] In 2003, the Committee adopted a *General Comment on 'adolescent health and development'* in the context of the CRC, which is based on a broad understanding of the concept 'health and development'.[131] On 17 September 2004, the Committee will hold a Day of General Discussion on 'Implementing child rights in early childhood'. In a preparatory document, the Committee emphasized that the right to survival and development in Article 6(2) can only be implemented in a holistic way by enforcing all other provisions recognized in the Convention, including the right to health, adequate nutrition and education: 'States Parties to the Convention need to ensure that in their first years all children have access to adequate health care and nutrition, as spelled out in article 24, to enable them to start a healthy life. In this

---

[130] CRC Committee, *o.c.* (note 99), paras. 93–98. See also R. Hodgkin and P. Newell, *o.c.* (note 28), pp. 625–635; G. Van Bueren, *o.c.* note 29, pp. 297–307; D. Parker and C. Sepúlveda, *o.c.* (note 123), pp. 69–106. See also CESCR Committee, *General Comment No. 14(2000) on the right to the highest attainable standard of health* (UN Doc. E/C.12/2000/4).
[131] CRC Committee, *o.c.* (note 87).

context breastfeeding, access to clean drinking water and adequate nutritious foods are vital'.[132]

76. Closely related to the right to health is the right of every child, pursuant to Article 27(1) of the CRC, to a 'standard of living adequate for the child's physical, mental, spiritual, moral and social development'. While recognizing in Article 27(2) the primary responsibility of the parents to secure, within their abilities and financial capacities, the conditions of living necessary for the child's development, States Parties are obliged by Article 27(3) to take appropriate measures to assist parents in case of need by providing material assistance and support programmes, particularly with regard to nutrition, clothing and housing. The identification of these three sub-elements of the right to an adequate standard of living corresponds to Article 11 of the CESCR. In 2002, the Committee on Economic, Social and Cultural Rights also derived the right to water from this umbrella social right.[133] In its General Guidelines for periodic reports, the CRC Committee requests States Parties to provide relevant information on targets, indicators and benchmarks in relation to nutrition, clothing and housing and on the progress achieved in implementing this right.[134] Typical indicators for nutrition, which also provide an indication for the implementation of the right to life, are:

- The percentage of infants with low birth weight;
- The percentage of children who are breastfed over a certain period of time;
- The percentage of children under five suffering from underweight, wasting and stunting;
- The percentage of households consuming iodized salt; and
- The Vitamin A supplementation coverage rate for the age between 6 and 59 months.[135]

77. The development of the child depends to a large extent on the enjoyment of the right to education. In Article 28 of the CRC, States Parties recognize the legal obligation to make primary education compulsory and available free to all,[136] and in the Millennium Development Goals of 2000, the Member States of the United Nations have pledged to achieve universal

---

[132] CRC Committee, Report on the Thirty-Fifth Session (UN Doc. CRC/C/137 2004), para. 8.

[133] CESCR Committee, General Comment No. 15(2002) on the right to water (UN Doc. E/C.12/2002/13).

[134] CRC Committee, o.c. (note 99), paras. 103–104.

[135] See UNICEF, o.c. (note 1), pp. 88–91.

[136] See also Articles 13 and 14 of the CESCR and CESCR Committee, General Comment No. 11(1999): Plans of action for primary education (UN Doc. E/C.12/1999/4) and General Comment No. 13(1999): The right to education (UN Doc. E/C.12/1999/10).

primary education by 2015. In addition, States Parties to the CRC shall make secondary education, including vocational education, available and accessible to every child and take appropriate measures such as the introduction of free education and offering financial assistance in case of need. Higher education shall be made accessible to all on the basis of capacity. Pursuant to Article 29 of the CRC, States Parties agree that the education of the child shall be directed to

- The development of the child's personality, talents and mental and physical abilities to their fullest potential;
- The development of respect for human rights;
- The development of respect for the child's parents and cultural identity;
- The preparation of the child for a life in a free society, in the spirit of understanding, peace, tolerance, equality of the sexes and friendship;
- The development of respect for the natural environment.

78.  These principal *aims of universal education*, which have been accepted as legally binding by almost all States of the world, promote, support and protect the core values of the CRC and are directly linked to the child's special developmental needs and diverse evolving capacities.[137] They also represent the ultimate goals that the holistic concept of the child's development wishes to achieve. Closely related to the aims and methods of education and the healthy development of children is the *right of the child to rest and leisure*, to engage in play and recreational activities appropriate to the age of the child and to participate freely in cultural life and the arts, as recognized by the States Parties in Article 31 of the CRC.

### 6.7.  *Right to Development and Eradication of Poverty*

79.  Although the reference to the *'development of the child'* in Article 6(2) of the CRC at first glance seems not to have to do anything with the general *human right to development*, as laid down in the 1986 *UN Declaration on the Right to Development*, a closer look might reveal certain similarities. First of all, the *travaux préparatoires* show that the concept of survival and development of the child was influenced by the development discourse of that time, which might be explained by the fact that the UN Declaration had been adopted only three years before the CRC. Secondly, the CRC Committee has pursued a holistic approach to the concept of development as rein-

---

[137] See also CRC Committee, *General Comment No. 1 on the aims of education* (UN Doc. CRC/GC/2001/1, 2001).

forcing all other provisions recognized in the Convention,[138] which is also expressed in the decision to regard Article 6 as one of the Convention's four general principles. In its General Guidelines for periodic reports, the Committee defines the development of the child, in close similarity to Principle 2 of the 1959 UN Declaration of the Rights of the Child, as 'including physical, mental, spiritual, moral, psychological and social development, in a manner compatible with human dignity, and to prepare the child for an individual life in a free society'.[139] This holistic concept of development is reinforced by the aims of education laid down in Article 29(1) of the CRC as outlined above.

80. If one compares these aims of education, which might be interpreted as the ultimate goals of a healthy development of the child, with the content of the human right to development, the similarities become evident. *Article 1 of the UN Declaration on the Right to Development* defines the right to development as

> 'an inalienable human right by virtue of which every human person and all peoples are entitled to participate in, contribute to, and enjoy economic, social, cultural and political development, in which all human rights and fundamental freedoms can be fully realized.'

81. In other words: the right to development has been characterized as a participatory process which ultimately shall lead to the full realization of all human rights and fundamental freedoms, the indivisibility and interdependence of which has been stressed in Article 6 of the Declaration. This holistic approach to human development has been reinforced by the legal obligation of almost all States of the world, pursuant to Article 6(2) of the CRC, to 'ensure to the maximum extent possible the survival and development of the child'. Only those States which fully comply with all civil, political, economic, social and cultural rights of the child guaranteed in the CRC can be considered as having ensured, 'to the maximum extent possible', the development of all children within their jurisdiction. If States create an environment that enables all children to grow up in a healthy and protected manner, free from fear and want,[140] and to develop their personality, talents

---

[138] See, *e.g.*, CRC Committee, *o.c.* (note 132), para. 8. See also R. Hodgkin and P. Newell, *o.c.* (note 28), p. 103; G. Van Bueren, *o.c.* (note 29), p. 293; M. Santos Pais, *o.c.* (note 28), p. 11.

[139] CRC Committee, *o.c.* (note 99), para. 40.

[140] These two important freedoms, first proclaimed by President Franklin D. Roosevelt, have been recognized in the 2nd preambular paragraph of the Universal Declaration of Human Rights.

and abilities to their fullest potential consistent with their evolving capacities, they at the same time implement the right to human development.

82. The overarching goal of the contemporary understanding of development is the *eradication of poverty*. In the Millennium Development Goals of 2000, the Member States of the UN have pledged, first of all, to eradicate extreme poverty and hunger by reducing by half the proportion of people living on less than a dollar a day and who suffer from hunger until the year 2015. Achieving universal primary education, reducing child mortality, improving maternal health, combating HIV/AIDS, malaria and other diseases, and ensuring environmental sustainability, *e.g.* by providing access to safe drinking water, constitute the most important elements of the overarching goal of eradicating poverty. A human rights approach to poverty reduction strategies, as promoted by the UN High Commissioner for Human Rights,[141] reinforces each of the eight development goals in the Millennium Declaration, as it is based on a universally recognized legal framework and, thereby, empowers the poor. In a rapidly globalizing world, effective poverty reduction requires concerted efforts of States and the *international community*, including global actors, such as the international donor community, international financial institutions and other intergovernmental and non-governmental organizations, as well as trans-national corporations.[142]

83. For a human rights approach to poverty reduction strategies, the CRC plays an important role, as it is the human rights treaty with the highest number of ratifications and broadest universal acceptance. In various provisions, the *CRC promotes international co-operation and assistance* to achieve the effective realization of the rights of the child.[143] With regard to *economic, social and cultural rights*, Article 4 contains a general obligation of States Parties to undertake all appropriate legislative, administrative and other measures, where needed, 'within the framework of international co-operation'. This general undertaking is further specified by the obligation to promote and encourage international co-operation aimed at the full real-

---

[141] *Cf.* Office of the High Commissioner for Human Rights, *Human Rights and Poverty Reduction— A Conceptual Framework* (New York and Geneva, United Nations, 2004); see also the '*Draft Guidelines: A Human Rights Approach to Poverty Reduction Strategies*', prepared by Paul Hunt, Manfred Nowak and Siddiq Osmani and published by the former High Commissioner Mary Robinson on 10 September 2002: http://www. unhchr.ch/development/povertyfinal.html (hereinafter *Draft Guidelines*).

[142] *Cf. Draft Guidelines* (note 141): 18: Monitoring and Accountability of Global Actors, paras. 241–249.

[143] *Cf. e.g.*, M. Santos Pais, *o.c.* (note 28), pp. 13–14.

ization of those rights that are most relevant to the right to life, survival and development of the child, such as the right to health in Article 24(4) and the right to education in Article 28(3). In this regard, particular account shall be taken of the needs of developing countries. One may, therefore, draw the conclusion that the obligation of States Parties under Article 6(2) to ensure 'to the maximum extent possible' the survival and development of the child does not only apply to children under the jurisdiction of the respective States Parties, but that it also creates an obligation to contribute to the healthy development of children in other countries by means of international co-operation and assistance. This conclusion reinforces the spirit of the UN Declaration on the Right to Development.